Claire Chennault
Amelia Earhart
Charles Lindbergh
Eddie Rickenbacker
Manfred von Richthofen
Chuck Yeager

Famous Flyers

Claire Chennault
Flying Tiger

Earle Rice Jr.

CHELSEA HOUSE
PUBLISHERS

A Haights Cross Communications Company

Philadelphia

Frontis: Claire Chennault would see many battles, both in the air against the enemy and on the ground against superiors who doubted his strategies, during his long and successful military career. He and his wife, Anna, are pictured here arriving at the Burbank airport in 1952 for a Flying Tigers reunion.

CHELSEA HOUSE PUBLISHERS

VP, NEW PRODUCT DEVELOPMENT   Sally Cheney
DIRECTOR OF PRODUCTION   Kim Shinners
CREATIVE MANAGER   Takeshi Takahashi
MANUFACTURING MANAGER   Diann Grasse

Staff for CLAIRE CHENNAULT

EXECUTIVE EDITOR   Lee Marcott
ASSOCIATE EDITOR   Bill Conn
PRODUCTION EDITOR   Jaimie Winkler
PICTURE RESEARCHER   Sarah Bloom
SERIES DESIGNER   Keith Trego
COVER DESIGNER   Keith Trego
LAYOUT   21st Century Publishing and Communications, Inc.

A Haights Cross Communications ✈ Company

http://www.chelseahouse.com

First Printing

1 3 5 7 9 8 6 4 2

Library of Congress Cataloging-in-Publication Data

Rice, Earle.
   Claire Chennault / by Earle Rice, Jr.
      p. cm.—(Famous flyers)
   Summary: Profiles Claire Lee Chennault who, after retiring from the United States
Army Air Corps, volunteered as an advisor to Chiang Kai-Shek and led both Chinese
and American air troops against Japan during World War II. Includes bibliographical
references and index.
   ISBN 0-7910-7217-7 HC   0-7910-7499-4 PB
   1. Chennault, Claire Lee, 1893–1958—Juvenile literature. 2. Generals—United
States—Biography—Juvenile literature. 3. United States. Army Air Forces—
Biography—Juvenile literature. 4. China. Kong jun. American Volunteer Group—
Biography—Juvenile literature. 5. World War, 1939–1945—Aerial operations,
American—Juvenile literature. [1. Chennault, Claire Lee, 1893–1958. 2. Air pilots.
3. Generals. 4. World War, 1939-1945—Aerial operations.] I. Title. II. Series.
   E745.C35 R53 2002
   940.54'4973'092—dc21
                                                                    2002014868

CONTENTS

A Lousy Way to Start a War

On the evening of July 7, 1937, a night awash in moonlight and pleasant summer breezes, a party from the American Embassy in Peking (now known as Beijing), China, embarked on a leisurely excursion across the calm waters of Pei Hai Lake near Peking's Forbidden City. Several Chinese boatmen poled along their lantern-lit barge with rhythmic ease. Members of the outing included U.S. Ambassador Nelson T. Johnson, military attaché Colonel Joseph W. Stilwell, Marine Embassy Guard commander Colonel John Marston, and their spouses. The ambassador had brought his guitar and entertained the group with song as the barge glided smoothly across the tranquil waters toward the marble tower of the White Dagoba, the Buddhist commemorative monument now gleaming softly in the moonlight. For a few engaging moments, the Americans slipped the bonds of reality and surrendered themselves completely to the storied charm of ancient Peking.

Reality returned, however, when another boat glided by carrying a group of Japanese officers. Prompted by their appearance, Colonel Marston commented that as senior officer of the foreign detachments, the Japanese had informed him of their plans to hold troop maneuvers that night at the railroad bridge at Lugouqiao, about 12 miles west of the city on the Peking–Hankow line. The railway represented the sole remaining gateway to Peking not under Japanese control. Lugouqiao formed a key rail junction where a branchline connected to Tianjin. Japanese maneuvers near

These Chinese soldiers keep watch behind a sandbag barricade on the Marco Polo Bridge. Gunfire exchanged with Japanese soldiers on this bridge led to full-scale war between China and Japan.

the junction during the previous two weeks had already given rise to unsettling speculations in the Chinese press.

Next to the railway bridge at Lugouqiao stands a stone bridge more than 800 years old. One of China's grandest monuments, it is adorned with marble lions and spans the Yongding River on 30 graceful arches. Named for the first Western admirer to cross over it in the 13th century, it is called the Marco Polo Bridge. Even as the ambassador's party lazed enjoyably on Pei Hai Lake, the bridge was about to take on a new—and infinitely more sinister—claim to fame.

As planned, Japanese troops commenced night maneuvers near the Marco Polo Bridge on the night of July 7, 1937. At 11:40 P.M., several shots rang out, shattering the stillness of the night in China and ultimately the peace of the world. A Japanese officer held a roll call of his troops and ostensibly discovered one private missing. The lieutenant in charge of the maneuvers led his troops across the bridge and proceeded directly to the gates of town. To the commander of the Chinese garrison posted in Lugouqiao, he said, "We demand to search the place. One of our men is missing." The Chinese captain denied his demand.

"You have no right," he countered, "just as you have no right to carry out your maneuvers here. I refuse."

The two officers exchanged no further words. Bullets precluded the need for more talk, fired first from the ranks of the Japanese soldiers and soon answered by the Chinese defenders. Soldiers on both sides fell dead in the confrontation that signified the start of what the Japanese euphemistically call the "China Incident" and what the Chinese more realistically refer to as their "War of Resistance." In retrospect, many students of 20th-century warfare point to the "incident" at the Marco Polo Bridge as the *true* beginning of World War II.

As the world watched passively and disinterestedly, the hostilities escalated rapidly and almost overnight turned into an unofficial shooting war. News of the war caught up with

Colonel Claire Lee Chennault two days later in Loyang (Luoyang) on July 9. Recently retired from the U.S. Army Air Corps as a captain, the new American adviser to the Chinese Air Force (CAF) had arrived in China barely more than a month earlier. He immediately wired his new employer in Nanking (Nanjing), Chinese Nationalist leader Generalissimo Chiang Kai-shek, offering his "services in any capacity he could use them." Under the circumstances—caught in a conflict between two foreign nations in a strange land—lesser men might have turned for home. But, as Chennault would put it later, "I never run from a fight." Few would find reason to doubt his courage when looking at Chennault's face, weathered and lined from years in an open cockpit; his dark eyes, deep-set and piercing; and his thin-lined mouth, sandwiched between a hawkish nose and a jutting chin that accentuated his determination.

Chennault received Chiang's answer in Sian (Xi'an) two days later: "Your voluntary offer of services gratefully accepted. Proceed to Nanchang. Direct final combat training fighter groups there." The generalissimo could not know it at the time, but he had just enlisted the aid of one of his greatest allies in China's battle against Japan.

While Chennault was assessing the fighting capabilities of the CAF, Chiang was evaluating the overall combat readiness of his armed forces from Kuling, his summer capital high among the pines in the mountains near Lake Poyang and the city of Nanchang. He did not like his findings. Chiang recognized that only a unified effort by all of the divided factions of China—Nationalists, Communists, and the multitudes controlled by warlords—would stand a chance of successfully opposing the professional army of modern Japan. He also recognized that if the Chinese chose to engage Japan in a declared war it would be a long and bitter one. But the choice was not his to make.

In early August, war fever gripped China. Students cried,

"It is better to be broken jade than whole tile," while newspapers urged, "Stand and fight; an end to compromise." Leaders of the dissident factions began flocking to Chiang's capital in Nanking to demand action. Chiang met with them at the Nanking Military Academy. Their demands carried a single message: Lead us against the Japanese and we pledge our troops and loyalty for the duration of the war. The generalissimo accepted their proposal, and China united for the first time in modern history.

Events began moving fast. On Wednesday, July 11, Chinese troops in Shanghai killed a Japanese officer and soldier and fighting broke out. Chiang held a war council meeting of Chinese military leaders, including Chennault, two days later on Friday the 13th. The Japanese threat to Shanghai forced the Chinese to disregard the fighting in the north and concentrate their defensive efforts to the south.

In mid-meeting, Chiang received a message. He read the message and handed it to Madame Chiang. Sobbing, she announced to the gathering in English, "They are shelling the Shanghai Civic Center. They are killing our people. They are killing our people." As she spoke, the cruiser *Idzumo* and other Japanese warships were pummeling the city from offshore positions in the Whangpoo (Huangpu) River.

Chennault asked, "What will you do now?"

Madame Chiang brushed her tears away and tossed her head back defiantly. "We will fight," she said.

The meeting broke up and Chiang's generals rushed here and there to prepare for battle. Madame Chiang asked Chennault to stay after the meeting. She questioned him about what kind of air action China could deliver against the Japanese the next day. He recommended dive-bombing and high-level bombing attacks on the Japanese warships that were providing the advancing enemy infantry with heavy artillery support. At that moment, Madame Chiang suddenly realized that she could not rely on a single Chinese air officer to plan and organize an air action of that size. She asked Chennault to take charge.

Chennault felt duty bound to honor her request. And he had trained a lifetime for just such a combat role. But with little time to prepare and with only the vaguest notion of the terrain and the opposing forces, the American airman found himself facing the greatest challenge of his career. Chennault and Billy McDonald—an old friend from his U.S. Army Air Corps days—drove at once to Chinese Air Force headquarters in Nanking and worked until 4:00 A.M., poring over maps and planning the bombing operation. "Unknowingly," Chennault would write later, "we were setting the stage for Shanghai's famous Black Saturday—a spectacle that shocked a world that was not yet calloused to mass murder from the sky by thousand-plane raids or atomic bombs."

Chennault found only two types of aircraft available for his use in the immediate vicinity of Nanking: American-built Curtiss Hawk III biplane fighters and Northrop 2EC monoplane light bombers. He decided to use the light bombers against the heavy cruiser *Idzumo*. The cruiser was anchored in the Whangpoo River, opposite the Japanese consulate at the edge of Shanghai's International Settlement. It represented the prime target as it housed Japanese naval headquarters for the region. Chennault would send the fighters against the remaining light cruisers in the stream. In his planning, he took great care to chart a course that would keep his planes from flying over the International Settlement. He wanted to avoid an international incident that would damage the Chinese cause in the event that something went wrong.

Four Northrop 2EC light bombers took to the air out of Nanking airfield at daybreak. They climbed to 7,500 feet (2,286 meters), leveled off, and set a course for Shanghai. Their mission: *sink the Idzumo.*

Chiang Kai-shek (left) and Claire Lee Chennault (right) formed a mutually beneficial alliance against the Japanese. Chiang received the services of an innovative air force leader, and Chennault got the opportunity to develop and institute a battle plan that would test his theories on air combat.

Despite Chennault's meticulous planning, the mission was doomed to failure from the start. Everything that could go wrong *did* go wrong. Bad weather was to prove key to the mission's bizarre outcome. Along the approach to target, an overcast sky obscured the city and everything around it. The inexperienced Chinese pilots struggled just to hold formation and keep up with their leader. When they arrived over target they could not see a hundred feet in any direction. To add to their woes, the gusts of a developing storm had blown them off course. The gods of war seemed to be playing tricks on them.

The weight of command bore heavily on the shoulders of the young flight leader. He was about to learn what leadership in combat is all about. It was decision time—and the decision was his alone to make. A more experienced pilot might have called off the mission and ordered his men back to base. But he was young and inexperienced. He chose instead to go on.

On his command, the four bombers dropped down through the thick cloud layer. At about 1,500 feet (457 meters), they finally broke into the clear. Directly below them lay Shanghai's International Settlement, a district that bordered the Whangpoo and was home to most of the city's European and American population. When they started their bombing run, they were positioned precisely where they were *not supposed to be.*

Chennault's inexperienced pilots soon sighted the blue-gray hulk of the *Idzumo* riding at anchor in the light brown waters of the Whangpoo. To call what happened next a tragedy would understate the event. The four bombers droned on to color the day black with high explosives and charred human flesh.

Before Chennault's arrival in China, Chinese pilots had undergone a type of ritualistic training that could best be described as too little and too rigid. The flying skills of most had advanced barely beyond the ability to take off and land. Instruction on proper bombing techniques concentrated on approaching targets at a fixed speed and altitude. Bombardiers were taught to release their bombs when a memorized picture of the target appeared in the bombsight. Rote training did little to prepare them for the unexpected. As might be expected, in the flush and fury of their first combat mission,

Chennault's newly acquired airmen failed to adjust to their changing situation.

Their instructions were to stay on a level-flight approach to their target at a height of 7,500 feet (2,286 meters). Instead, they dropped down in a shallow dive toward the enemy warships below. All four bombardiers, lacking composure and presence of mind, released their bombs as soon as the memorized picture of the *Idzumo* appeared in their bombsights—which was much too soon. Not one of them had remembered to reset his bombsight to adjust for the differences in speed, height, and angle of attack. As a result, hundreds of Chinese suffered for the mental lapses of a few.

Of all the world's streets, perhaps none is so thickly trafficked as Shanghai's Nanking Road. On that morning, tens of thousands of refugees were pouring into the settlement from Chapei and parts of Kiangsu (Jiangsu) Province, fleeing the areas being pounded by Japanese guns. Thousands of them took heart when four Chinese planes broke through the cloud cover above them. But twin feelings of disbelief and horror dashed their lifted spirits when they saw two 1,100-pound bombs plummeting down upon them. Unbelievably, their own planes were bombing them.

Both bombs smashed into their midst. They struck not far from the Cathay Hotel, a popular gathering place for a wealthy, mostly Western, class of clientele. Through some twist of fate, the first bomb impacted without going off. The second bomb exploded with shattering force. Concussion waves shook the earth. Life-destroying chunks of hot metal whizzed through the air. The blast killed 950 people and badly injured 1,100 more. In the skies above, the Chinese airmen heard none of the shrieks of the maimed and dying far below them. They pressed on resolutely with their mission to sink the *Idzumo*.

Their minds now intent only upon destroying the enemy cruiser, the inept airmen steadily closed distance with the

There were hundreds of dead and injured on busy Nanking Road in Shanghai after Chinese pilots mistakenly bombed their own territory.

hulking blue-gray vessel. They drew so near as to make missing it with their remaining bombs all but impossible. Yet miss it they did. The *Idzumo* came through the attack unharmed. Several smaller Japanese warships anchored nearby also escaped without a nick.

When the last Chinese bomb exploded harmlessly in the Whangpoo, the bombers turned for home. The airmen had failed miserably. Their failure would cause much shame to fall upon the houses of their fathers. Surely their ancestors would seethe with anger—not to mention the American called Chennault. On top of all this, a final embarrassment was still to come. It came in the form of a report from a warship that had suffered wide damage from broken glass caused by their errant bombs. The vessel filing the report was the U.S. cruiser *Augusta*.

Earlier that morning, Claire Chennault had risen after only a few hours sleep and taken off from Nanking in an unarmed Curtiss Hawk 75 to watch the attack on Shanghai as a "neutral" observer. The 75, a sleek monoplane, was the first single-winger in the famous Hawk family of fighter planes. Madame Chiang had reserved it for Chennault's personal use. He flew down the Yangtze River Valley and soon ran into the same lowered ceiling and gusty winds that had plagued his bombers a little earlier.

The veteran pilot had about lost hope of breaking through the murk to Shanghai when he "spotted a flight of three Chinese planes reforming over the [Yangtze] river and another trio climbing fast." Below them he could see a warship steaming off at full speed with white foam curving off its bow, thick black smoke billowing from its smokestacks, and a string of gunfire flashes blinking along its gray decks. The Chinese planes had been dive-bombing the fleeing vessel. Chennault dropped lower to identify the ship:

> I came up low behind the smoke, pulled up for a quick look, and saw, amid the flashing of her machine guns, a huge Union Jack [British flag] painted on the afterdeck. It was the British cruiser *Cumberland*.

Chennault made a second pass by the warship to confirm its identity then "headed full throttle for Nanking," convinced that "another international incident was brewing." It was not until somewhere on the flight home that he had time to observe the holes in both wings—bullet holes. Back at Nanking, he pointed out the holes to his armament specialist and snarled, "Get some guns on this ship and get 'em on in a hurry." Chennault's days as a neutral observer were over. The next time someone shot at him, he meant to shoot back.

Chennault was mad, perhaps madder than he had ever been before. And why not? He had carefully planned a payback bombing mission that failed through no fault of his own. His inexperienced pilots had simply not executed. Because of their failings, hundreds of innocent Chinese lay dead in the streets of Shanghai, a British warship was mistakenly attacked, and two international incidents were in the making. If that were not enough for one day, he had barely escaped unscathed from friendly fire. Who would blame the American commander for thinking that this was a lousy way to start a war?

Evolution of a Fighter Pilot

Some men are born to do what others only dream of. Such a man was Claire Lee Chennault. His war in China began on Shanghai's Black Saturday and lasted for eight long years. After an inauspicious beginning, he went on to become a living legend in defense of a far-off land that he came to love. The Chennault legend began with Claire's birth in Commerce, Texas, on September 6, 1893, and soon shifted to the bayou country of northeastern Louisiana.

The oldest son of John Stonewall Jackson Chennault and his young wife Jessie Lee, Claire entered life with a name guaranteed to develop his fighting skills at a very young age. His maternal uncle and namesake—18-year-old deputy sheriff Claire Lee— had been overpowered and shot to death by a prisoner in his custody shortly before the birth of his nephew. On his father's side, the name of Chennault boasted a heritage of fierce pride and free spirits. His family worked hard, played hard, and never flinched from a fight. The second Claire Lee would grow up entertaining no illusions that life would be a lark.

Claire, along with his younger brother Billy, spent his early years discovering the wonders of hunting and fishing—

The boy born Claire Lee Chennault in Commerce, Texas, would grow up to be the highly competitive "Old Man," as he was called by the pilots of the AVG. Both Chennault and the Flying Tigers had an enormous impact on China's war with Japan.

while developing a sense of total freedom and self-reliance—in the deep woods and backwaters near his boyhood home on the Bayou Macon. He became at one with the wild country, tutoring himself in survival training and honing his skills as an expert marksman. Swamps infested with water moccasins held no fear for Chennault. He thought nothing of sharing their watery environment wearing only a pair of swim trunks. On one occasion he told a companion that snakes did not bother him nor he them. "You just slap the water," he explained. "They will go away, unless of course, it's mating season." He did not explain what happened next.

Early in life, Chennault's stern but loving family taught him discipline and the value of working hard and meeting life on its own terms. Then tragedy struck him at the age of eight when his mother contracted tuberculosis and died. Deeply saddened, young Claire drew within himself and waged a private battle against feelings of loneliness and isolation. His only social activities and sense of community came through the Baptist Church, school, and the local baseball team. Through these outside connections, he grew devoutly religious, became a fine scholar, and developed into an excellent athlete.

Chennault's father married again when Claire was 12 years old. John's new spouse was Lottie Barnes, who had been Claire's teacher in grade school. "His choice of a wife could not have been better," Chennault wrote later, "for I had already learned to love her." Lottie became not only a "new" mother to him but a best friend as well. She taught him to want to be the best at whatever he tried. Furthermore, she impressed upon him the importance of seeking a good education.

Of French Huguenot stock, and related paternally to Sam Houston and maternally to Robert E. Lee, it comes as no surprise that young Claire should begin dreaming of a military career. Lottie supported his dream. On January 25, 1909, he entered Louisiana State University (LSU) in Baton Rouge at the age of 14, which was typical for the early 20th century. He had selected LSU because its curriculum required military training. Chennault immediately fell victim to the usual hazing indignities practiced by the more-privileged upper classmen. He reacted to their harassment with self-confidence and a strong will, characteristics that he would carry with him throughout all his days.

Tragedy struck Chennault again when Lottie died on November 28, 1909, just as he was completing his second semester. "I was alone again," Chennault wrote years later, "and really never found another companion whom I could so completely admire, respect, and love." Lottie's death, coupled with that of his mother, left a void in his life that he never managed to fill completely. The loss of his second mother, along with the strain on the family finances, strongly influenced his decision not to return to LSU.

Still drawn toward a military career, and with an eye toward relieving the tuition strain on the family budget, Chennault investigated the possibilities of an appointment to either the Military Academy at West Point or the Naval Academy at Annapolis. On day two of a three-day testing period at the Naval Academy, he learned that midshipmen are not allowed off the academy grounds during their first two years. Unwilling to surrender his freedom for that long, he returned home. "Sight of the grim gray walls on the Severn [River] chilled my enthusiasm to become an admiral," he explained.

Spirits may thrive on freedom but stomachs need sustenance. As a way of keeping food on the dinner table, Chennault reached out to the teaching profession. After completing a stint for credits at a state teacher's college at Natchitoches, he accepted a position at a one-room school in Athens, Louisiana. In Athens, Chennault doubled as a baseball coach and did an impressive job with a tough bunch of students. He jokingly pointed out that his major qualification for the job was that he "was still a minor and could legally commit assault and battery on the unruly students. . . . It took a few stiff sessions with bare knuckles behind the schoolhouse to clinch the job."

Chennault grew to love teaching, but he found it difficult to live on his small salary. It became even more difficult when love came along. In the spring of 1910, he met Nell Thompson, who delivered the valedictorian address at a high school where his uncle was principal. While courting his new love that summer, he found a second love when he laid eyes on an airplane for the first time at the Louisiana State Fair in Shreveport—a Curtiss pusher biplane. The urge to fly owned him from that day forward. Chennault married Nell on Christmas Day 1911. But he would have to wait several more years to fulfill his urge to fly.

After the arrival of the first two of an eventual eight children, the pressures of providing for his family forced him to move from one teaching job to another in several states—Mississippi, Kentucky, Tennessee, and Ohio—always seeking a higher salary. In 1917, his struggles finally brought him to Akron, Ohio, where he accepted a factory job.

When the United States entered World War I against Germany in April 1917, Chennault applied at once for army flight training, hoping to learn to fly at government expense. By then, however, he was almost 24—old for a fledgling pilot—and the father of three. The army rejected his application, noting, "Applicant does not possess necessary qualifications for a successful aviator." But there *was* a war on, and the army needed infantry officers. They assigned Chennault to Officers Training School at Fort

Chennault learned to fly the Curtiss Company's Jenny at the army's Kelly Field in San Antonio, Texas. The plane was used as a basic trainer by the army and navy.

Benjamin Harrison, Indiana, where he earned the silver bars of a first lieutenant in the infantry reserve in 90 days.

The army ordered the newly commissioned lieutenant to Fort Travis in San Antonio, Texas. Located not far away in the same city was a new base called Kelly Field. In November 1917, it was the only base in the country for training pilots. Chennault soon arranged a transfer to the new airfield. Befriending some of the flying instructors at Kelly Field, he cajoled them into to giving him informal flying lessons in the Curtiss JN-4, the famous "Jenny." He managed to log more than 80 flying hours that way. But his lessons were cut short when new orders whisked him off to

Langley Field, Virginia, to help forestall a revolt of angry African–American construction troops.

After calm was restored to the Virginia base, Chennault contracted influenza—the great epidemic of that era—and almost died. A medical officer isolated him in an outbuilding reserved for the dying. When a nurse protested that he was not dead yet, the doctor replied, "He will be before morning." But somehow Chennault lived through the night. Through perpetual adversities, Chennault persevered and kept applying for formal flight training. The army finally rewarded his bulldog-like tenacity when the war ended in 1918 and reassigned him to Kelly Field. During his informal flight training he had picked up some bad habits and now had to struggle to overcome them, but he finally earned the right to pin on the silver wings of a fighter pilot. Unfortunately, his long-held dream of becoming a pilot came true at precisely the wrong time. Now that the war had been won, the army needed fewer pilots. Fighter pilot Chennault, discharge in hand, returned to Louisiana on April 16, 1920.

But Chennault was not to be grounded so easily. Flying was all he had ever really wanted to do. "I have tasted of the air," he wrote to his father, "and I cannot get it out of my craw." He wasted no time in applying for a commission in the army's newly formed Air Service (which had taken over the aviation function from the Signal Corps) and was accepted with the regular commission of first lieutenant. Less than three months after his discharge, he returned to active duty.

On July 1, 1920, Chennault reported to Ellington Field, Texas, to undergo training in the army's first course in aerial fighting tactics. The course—taught by the likes of Carl Spaatz and other notable airmen destined to become famous in World War II—stressed the one-on-one dogfighting techniques used in World War I. Chennault excelled in these lessons but began to think about better ways of winning in the air. His ideas involved flying tight formations and working in teams—tactics that he would introduce later in China. For the present, however, the army put Chennault's ideas on hold when two planes collided in midair.

In 1923, Hawaii called to Chennault and his family, which

The Air Service

The U.S. Army began developing a military capability in the air with the use of balloons in the Civil War and later in the Spanish-American War. The balloons provided a lofty platform from which observers could watch enemy troop movements and direct artillery fire. On August 1, 1907, the army created an Aeronautical Division of the Signal Corps, which evolved into the Aeronautical Section of the Signal Corps with an act of Congress on July 18, 1914.

The army's first military use of the airplane came in an unsuccessful effort against Mexican revolutionary Pancho Villa in 1916. A year later, the United States entered World War I with one poorly equipped air unit, burgeoning by war's end to 195,000 officers and enlisted personnel, 45 squadrons, and 750 planes. On May 20, 1918, an executive order removed aviation from the Signal Corps and established the Army Air Service.

After World War I, the Air Service demobilized rapidly and cut back to a fraction of its wartime strength. Brigadier General William Mitchell, who had directed U.S. air operations in France during the war, campaigned for the creation of a separate air force equivalent to the army and navy. Instead, Congress enacted the Army Reorganization Act of 1920, which established the Air Service as a combatant unit within the army. In 1926, the Air Corps Act replaced the Air Service with the Army Air Corps.

On June 20, 1941, the Army Air Forces supplanted the Army Air Corps and gained self-governing status within the army. The following March, all army air units were merged into the Army Air Forces (AAF) under a single commander, General Henry H. "Hap" Arnold. With the passage of the National Security Act on July 26, 1947, the air service finally achieved total independence as the U.S. Air Force.

then included six boys. Chennault assumed command of the Nineteenth Fighter Squadron—called the Fighting Cocks—at Luke Field in Pearl Harbor. He compared his first command to a boy's first love: "[B]igger and better things may come his way later, but there is always a special place in his heart for the first." And with love and hard-driving ways, Chennault molded the Fighting Cocks into the best fighter squadron in the army. Eager to prove the worth of their new air service, his squadron quickly developed a rivalry with the army artillery and the navy in the islands.

On one occasion, Chennault—now lean, tan, fit, and sporting a jaunty mustache—led his Fighting Cocks on a mock dive-bombing and strafing attack against army artillery positions. Flying Thomas-Morse MB–3 biplanes (the first American-built fighter plane), they swooped down on wary army gunners like nothing the artillerymen had ever seen before. Chennault's attackers sent the gunners scampering for cover. And they colored more than a few faces red among the army's top brass, most of whom favored the tried-and-true ground forces over the newer, untested air service. In recognition of his successful exercise, the army rewarded him with a week's confinement to base. Not a bad price to pay, Chennault felt, for a chance to test his tactics.

Chennault and his Fighting Cocks later took on the navy during war games in 1925. Well trained in aerobatics and team play, they overcame a navy dive-bomber squadron with amusing ease—an amusement not shared by certain high-level navy commanders who refused to let go of yesterday's tactics and strategies. (Tactics involve the art of positioning or maneuvering forces skillfully in battle; strategy is the plan, or planning, for an entire operation of a war or military campaign.) Chennault's fame started to spread in military circles.

In 1926 the period that Chennault later described as

"my happiest time in the Air Corps" came to an end when he received transfer orders back to Texas, this time to Brooks Field as a flight instructor. At Brooks, he continued to develop and test his ideas about aerial combat. Chennault's work there led directly to his promotion to captain and to his next duty assignment at the Air Corps Tactical School. His career path as a fighter pilot was still on track—but turbulence loomed just ahead.

Letter from the Orient

When Captain Chennault arrived at Air Corps Tactical School at Langley Field, Virginia, in 1931, he started to sense that his best years as a career pilot were behind him. There would be more good times ahead of him, but none so free from care as the times now past. Chennault's growing obsession with the tactics of air warfare, and his outspoken ways of advancing his opinions, were not well calculated to enhance his career path. His troubled years began.

In Hawaii, Chennault had already encountered his share of run-ins with top-level brass in both the army and the navy. At Langley, he found himself on the losing side of a bitter service debate that was to keep him in hot water for almost the next decade. Two schools of thought about the future of air warfare existed at the time. Mainstream thinkers championed the bomber as the fundamental air weapon of the future. In the early 1930s, they subscribed to the concepts put forth by Italian General Giulio Douhet in his book *The War of 194–* and considered the heavily armed bomber invulnerable to attack. The book, as Chennault wrote later, "became the strategic bible of the Air Corps." It "painted a brilliant picture of great bomber fleets fighting their way unescorted to targets, with the enemy fighters and flak [bursting antiaircraft shells] impotent in the face of their fury." Advances in design had produced bombers that flew as fast as fighters and carried twice their

The Forbidden City in Peking was at one time an enclosed area with buildings that were only accessible to China's imperial families. Chennault's military career was about to take a turn because of shots fired between Japan and China on the Marco Polo Bridge south of the Forbidden City.

armaments—such as the Martin B-10—and lent credence to Douhet's theories.

Conversely, Chennault, and a minority of fighter-plane advocates, thought that the notion of the bomber's invulnerability was rubbish. While not opposed to the bomber, Chennault insisted that bombers were susceptible to attack by fighters. Strongly influenced by his study of air operations in World War I, he believed that bombers could not operate effectively until air superiority was established. Whether operating against incoming enemy bombers, or against enemy fighters threatening outgoing American bombers, only fighters trained to "destroy hostile enemy aircraft" could win air superiority.

But the odds were stacked against Chennault and his theories. "The neglected field of fighter tactics," he noted later, "together with the total lack of any means for obtaining information about the enemy and tracking his airplanes, made the contest then even more unequal." Opposition to his theories continued at the training school.

Chennault found himself immediately at odds with the fighter tactics taught by his new flying instructor, Clayton Bissell, a World War I fighter ace. (An ace was—and still is—a pilot with five or more confirmed victories or kills.) Bissell taught, in Chennault's words, the "dawn-patrol and dogfight tactics of the Western Front [which] were so inadequate against the new bombers that Bissell had virtually abandoned the idea that fighters could shoot down bombers." Chennault made a point of bringing that simple fact to Bissell's attention whenever the opportunity arose during his training. His observations did little to endear him to his instructor, who would enjoy the last laugh years later.

After graduation, Chennault stayed on with the school as a senior instructor in fighter tactics. In 1931 he moved to Maxwell Field, Alabama, where he dedicated himself to modernizing fighter tactics for the next five years. His interest in World War I had led him to respect the work of German ace Oswald Boelcke, whom many consider to be the first great tactician of air fighting. One of the German ace's pioneering discoveries particularly impressed Chennault: "Two planes could be maneuvered to fight together as a team." More important, perhaps, Boelcke grasped the importance of his discovery.

Giulio Douhet: Father of Controversy

Born into a family of Napoleonic military officers in 1869, Douhet has been described as arrogant, visionary, and tactless. As an airpower theorist, he became nothing less than a father of controversy. In the family tradition, Douhet took a commission as a second lieutenant in the artillery in 1892. He became involved in the fledgling Italian air service after publishing his first paper on military aviation in 1909.

Douhet commanded the world's first bombardment unit in Libya during the Italo-Turkish War in 1911. At the outbreak of World War I, he served as chief of staff of an infantry division but was appointed head of the army's aviation section in 1915. His brash personality soon earned him a court-martial and a year in prison for criticizing army leaders in cabinet memoranda late in the year. After Italian military reverses in Caporetto, he was recalled and appointed head of the Central Aeronautical Bureau.

His chief claim to world renown came with the publication of his famous book *Il Dominio dell' Aria (The Command of the Air)* in 1921 and several smaller works on the subject of airpower. He envisioned aircraft as the ultimate offensive weapon, against which he saw no effective defense. And he foresaw the use of bombers that would strike at enemy cities, industries, and transport networks, while wreaking havoc with civilian populaces. His book *The War of 194–* stirred a fighter-vs.-bomber controversy in the U.S. military community that raged for two decades after World War I.

Douhet never intended his theories—some right and some wrong—for universal consumption. But his futuristic imaginings fathered controversy around the globe during the first half of the 20th century. In 1922, Douhet served briefly as commissioner of aviation in Mussolini's Fascist government and then retired. He died in 1930.

Boelcke based his thinking on an old military axiom that states: All other factors being equal, the difference in firepower between opposing forces lies not simply in the difference in the number of guns on each side, but rather in the *square* of the difference when those guns are concentrated. Simply put, two planes attacking together deliver the same firepower as four planes attacking individually. For the rest of his career, Chennault would shun individual dogfighting tactics and build on Boelcke's rules of team fighting.

Through his studies and by practical application in the air, Chennault concluded that the Air Corps' standard three-plane "vee" formation was too unwieldy for air fighting in a fast-paced modern environment. Instead, he introduced a looser, two-plane element consisting of a leader and a wingman, which effectively combined increased flexibility with concentrated firepower (Boelcke's square). He took full advantage of his position as flight instructor to test his theories and to check out every new fighter plane that appeared on the scene—Curtiss P-6s and Boeing P-12s and P-26s.

Chennault stressed teamwork and the importance of surprise and aggressive flying. He taught his pilots to keep control of the fight by maintaining superior airspeed and altitude—dive and climb. A good pilot must learn to recognize when textbook solutions do not apply and to trust his own gut feelings. And he must respect the value of running and living to fight again when outnumbered or otherwise disadvantaged.

Chennault's critics conceded that his fighter tactics were sound but were quick to question their effectiveness against bombers in a sky whose vastness alone made it all but impossible for the fighters to find them. They pointed to Air Corps maneuvers in Ohio in 1931, in which the fighter commander failed to intercept any bombers during two weeks of action. The general in charge of the maneuvers concluded: "Due to increased speeds and limitless space, it is impossible for fighters to intercept bombers and therefore it is inconsistent with the employment of air force to develop fighters." Chennault disagreed, attributing the lack of interceptions to the fighter commander's improper employment of his aircraft. But Chennault recognized the need for some kind of early warning network.

In 1932, in California, Henry "Hap" Arnold, then a lieutenant colonel and later the commanding general of the U.S. Army Air Force, sent squadrons of B-10s from San Diego to bomb March Field in a similar exercise. Squadrons of defending fighters at the airbase took off according to strict military procedures. Instead of scrambling to become airborne, the fighters rose unhurriedly and circled over the field until all of the squadrons had formed up. By then, the bombers had already come and gone. Arnold concluded from this mock attack that fighters would be ineffective in a wartime situation. He sent a report of his conclusions to the tactical school for comment.

In an eight-page rebuttal to his report, Chennault criticized the performance of the fighters and the conclusions reached by Arnold. The future commander of the U.S. Air Force wrote back to the school asking, "Who is this damned fellow Chennault?" Chennault had added another name to his growing list of detractors.

Chennault's faith in the fighter plane remained unshaken. He studied English and German early warning systems and added his own improvements. Writing of those days later, he noted that the "biggest problem of modern fighters was intelligence." He advocated establishing early warning nets to track hostile aircraft and furnish fighters with the information and time needed to intercept them. "Without a continuous stream of accurate information keeping the fighters posted on exactly where the high-speed bombers

Henry "Hap" Arnold played an essential role in building the air force into a powerful entity during World War II. Arnold and Chennault had opposing views on the use of air fighters in battle.

were, attempts at interception were like hunting needles in a limitless haystack." In a later air exercise held in 1933, Chennault cut the haystack down to size.

He helped prepare a warning network covering 16,000

square miles (41,440 square kilometers), spread across 69 army posts stretching from Dayton, Ohio, to Fort Knox, Kentucky. Aircraft spotters at each post reported by telephone and radio to the fighter operations center at Louisville. Fighters from Louisville successfully intercepted and "attacked" bombers flying from Dayton—at both high and low altitudes—long before they reached Fort Knox. The net proved so effective that the bomber supporters claimed "unfair conditions" and initiated operational limitations on the defending interceptors.

In 1933, Chennault wrote a paper entitled *The Role of Defensive Pursuit*, which defined all of the principles and factors related to the use of defensive aircraft, from single-seat fighters to modern-day jets and missiles. The army never really accepted it, but the mimeographed text formed the cornerstone of an early warning and interception system that would yield incredible results in China a few years later.

Chennault now had something to boast about and he complained loudly to all those "bomber boys" who could not—or would not—share his vision of the fighter's role in the next war—a war that was already taking shape in Europe. In November 1935, he was summoned to appear before a commission studying the role of military aviation. He finally had a platform from which to voice his controversial views. And speak out he did.

In his abrasive testimony, he attacked an army general's handling of a maneuver held in New Jersey a year earlier, in which the general had severely restricted the use of airpower. The general defended his actions on the spot, maintaining that he had handled the exercise in the best possible manner.

Captain Chennault snapped back at the general. "General," he said, obstinately and unburdened by tact, "if that is the best you can do in the way of planning for future wars, perhaps it is time for the Air Corps to take over." Another name went on the list of Chennault's detractors. And his own name was removed from the list of candidates for the Army's Command and General Staff School, which for all practical purposes signaled the end of his first Air Corps career.

Faced with a growing opposition to his theories, and likely sensing that his career was drawing to a close, Chennault began lashing out at his superiors and detractors. His superiors eventually pronounced him no longer suited to the role of an instructor. But his flying skills had not diminished. Although no longer valued as an instructor, he was still one of the hottest pilots around. And the opportunity to prove it came to him by chance.

Major General John Curry, commanding officer of the tactical school, described Chennault as "a fearless pilot, an able air leader, and one of the outstanding authorities on pursuit aviation." In 1932, General Curry had witnessed a performance by the Hell Divers, the navy's three-plane aerial acrobatic team. Although impressed by their precision flying, he thought at the time that his pilots could do anything the navy could do—only better. To Chennault's delight, Curry now turned to him to help prove the point.

Chennault put together a three-man flying team made up of himself and two of the best pilots he knew—Second Lieutenant Haywood "Possum" Hansell and Sergeant John H. "Luke" Williamson. Hansell would later serve as a wing commander in Europe during World War II. Williamson was Chennault's former student at Brooks Field. Hansell was to stay with the original trio for a year, after which Billy McDonald, another sergeant pilot, replaced him.

Inspired by a popular song of the day, the trio dubbed themselves "Three Men on a Flying Trapeze." Flying Boeing P-12Es, they staged air shows all around the nation, developing into a crack flying team and attracting crowds by the

The army's "Three Men on a Flying Trapeze" impressed spectators with their precision maneuvers at air shows around the country. Chennault (center) saw this success as proof that pilots could execute complex moves in teams during battle.

thousands. During three years of precision flying exhibitions, they performed "every acrobatic maneuver in the books and some that weren't, all in perfect formation." And in so doing, they provided "convincing proof of Boelcke's theory that fighters could battle together through the most violent maneuvers of combat."

In January 1936 the team flew one last performance at the Pan-American Air Show in Miami, Florida. Once more, chance intervened in the life of Claire Chennault. Among the spectators that day was General Mow Pang Tsu of the Chinese Air Force. Chennault's team greatly impressed the general. Later that day, William Pawley, an aviation entrepreneur who had been selling airplanes to the Chinese for years, invited the trio to his yacht so that Mow could meet them. Mow asked Williamson and McDonald to come to China to serve as much-needed flight instructors.

The two sergeants, who also held reserve commissions as second lieutenants, had recently applied for regular commissions, competing with more than 400 candidates for 52 openings. Chennault described the pair as outstanding pilots and praised their character. "If I was going to war," he wrote, "and I were ordered to the front, I would choose these two men to accompany me into combat, and that is the highest compliment a combat-formation leader can pay." But neither man had more than two years of college, and, on that account, the army turned down their applications.

Angry, Chennault advised them to accept Mow's offer, leaving open the prospect that he might join them later. Williamson and McDonald took his advice and sailed for China that summer. The pair would soon become Chennault's bridge to the Orient—and to an honored place in history.

Through the remainder of 1936 and on into the next year, Chennault's health and morale declined. He felt that he had outlived his usefulness to the Air Corps and admitted to a friend that his "heart was no longer in the fight." Suffering from exhaustion and low blood pressure, and permanently grounded because of impaired hearing and chronic bronchitis, he knew that time was running out on his Air Corps career. The army sent him to a hospital in Hot Springs, Arkansas, where he began contemplating his future.

When the army suggested retirement, he decided to accept the offer. He received several flattering proposals from aircraft manufacturers, but he felt "no urge to fly a desk." Yet, as he surely must have asked himself, what else was there? His answer came in the spring of 1937, in a letter from the Orient.

Birth of
a Legend

With war clouds gathering over China in the spring of 1937, Generalissimo Chiang Kai-shek's need for a well-trained air force spurred him into looking for outside help. He assigned to his spouse the job of searching out an experienced adviser who had courage and good character. Madame Chiang, a brilliant and strong-willed woman educated in the United States, contacted Claire Chennault through Roy Holbrook, a former Air Corps officer and friend of the aging airman. Holbrook was then serving as confidential adviser to the Central Trust Company of China.

Madame Chiang wanted Chennault to conduct a three-month confidential survey of the Chinese Air Force (CAF). She was prepared to offer Chennault "$1,000 a month plus expenses, a car, chauffeur, and interpreter, and the right to fly any plane in the Chinese Air Force." Would he accept? He would.

At midnight on April 30, 1937, after settling his family on the shores of Lake St. John near Waterproof, Louisiana, and after the Air Corps had pronounced him "incapacitated for active service on account of disability," Chennault officially retired from the U.S. Army with the rank of captain. On the morning of May 1, 1937, he headed for San Francisco where he boarded the Dollar Line's *President Garfield* and embarked— China bound—on the greatest adventure of his life.

En route to China, the *President Garfield* put into port at Kobe, Japan, for a brief layover. Billy McDonald, Chennault's old pal from their "Flying Trapeze" days, met him at the dock. McDonald was traveling on a passport that listed his occupation as assistant manager of a troupe of acrobats. The two friends spent the next few days touring Japan, viewing its sights "through the eyes of experienced airmen gauging

Chiang Kai-shek (in uniform) met with Japan's ambassador to China, Shigero Kawagoye (right) and members of their staffs in Nanking, China, in late 1936. The meeting failed to stop Japan's invasion of China.

potential targets" and taking innumerable photographs with cameras concealed under their topcoats.

Besides Kobe, they visited the cities of Kyoto and Osaka, then sailed down the Inland Sea. Along the way, they observed shipping routes, war industries, and other potential targets, documenting their travels with countless notes and photographs. After stopovers in the seaport cities of Shimonoseki and Moji (Kitakyushu), they sailed across the Yellow Sea for Shanghai. Between them—as Chennault was to learn four years later—the two pals had compiled more Japanese target information than was contained in U.S. War Department intelligence files.

The two amateur spies arrived in Shanghai in early June. Soon afterward, on a sultry afternoon, Roy Holbrook appeared at Chennault's quarters to escort him to the French Concession where he was to meet his new employer—Madame Chiang. When "a vivacious young girl clad in a modish Paris frock tripped into the room, bubbling with energy and enthusiasm," Chennault took her to be a young friend of Roy's and remained seated.

Imagine Chennault's surprise when Roy poked him and said, "Madame Chiang, may I present Colonel Chennault?"

Madame Chiang spoke perfect English in a rich southern drawl. Her beauty, soft voice, and charm completely captivated the rough-cut captain from the bayous. Of her, he wrote in his diary that night, "She will always be a princess to me." Through long years of defeat and victory, his esteem for her never wavered or waned.

On Madame Chiang's instructions, Chennault set out on a 90-day inspection tour of the CAF and its facilities, starting in Nanking. He did not like what he found. Years of graft and inept management, along with inferior aircraft and the lack of credible leadership, had left China's air service in little more than a shambles. In 1932 an unofficial American mission headed by Colonel Jack Jouett had established military flight schools patterned after U.S. flight-training programs. But after Jouett had laid the foundation for the CAF, his mission ended on a sour note when the United States refused to help the Central Government suppress a rebellion in Fukien Province by bombing rebel forces.

The U.S.–China split coincided with Italy's attempt to corner the aviation market in China. After Jouett's departure, the Italians stocked the CAF with inferior Italian-built aircraft and operated flying schools that awarded pilot's wings to anyone who survived the training. Chennault discovered that the number of combat-ready aircraft hovered around 100 rather than the 500 listed by the CAF commissioners on their rolls. On July 7, 1937, the incident between Japanese and Chinese soldiers at the Marco Polo Bridge cut short Chennault's tour.

After Chiang Kai-shek accepted Chennault's offer to serve China, as described in Chapter 1, Chennault proceeded to Nanchang to take command of the air-training activities there. "Combat training at Nanchang was a nightmare I will never forget," he wrote later. He found the food bad, the weather worse—dust storms one day, rain the next. Except for a handful of Boeing P-26s, none of the CAF's aircraft could match up with superior Japanese makes. Worse yet, most of the Italian-trained pilots could barely pilot their planes off the ground without crashing. And landings constituted a total catastrophe.

When Generalissimo Chiang later asked Chennault if China's air force was ready for war, Chennault responded with a resounding "no." His honesty, even though his answer was far from what Chiang wanted to hear, earned Chennault the complete trust of China's leader for the rest of their years together.

Following the *Idzumo* fiasco, China's immediate need for skilled pilots became painfully apparent. Soviet-supplied pilots and planes helped to blunt the Japanese advances

Japanese troops, such as those shown here in 1938, continued to gain ground in China's cities and villages. In 1941 the United States unofficially lent its support to China with the formation of the American Volunteer Group.

temporarily, but Soviet aid amounted to little more than applying a bandage to a gaping wound. Madame Chiang suggested that Chennault might want to seek help from men who fly and fight for pay—*mercenaries*. He opposed her suggestion, fearing that such an offer from China might attract mostly scoundrels and misfits. In the fall of 1938, however, aviation entrepreneur William Pawley offered to sell 24 long-range Vultee V-11 bombers to China. They would need pilots to fly them. Chennault was forced to agree to the mercenaries.

With few exceptions, Chennault got exactly what he expected—scoundrels and misfits, who "subsisted almost entirely on high-octane beverages." Most could not pass muster as disciplined military pilots. Many of the "mercs" established Hankow's Dump Street—a garish nightclub district replete with dance-hall girls, cheap booze, dope dealers, and spies—as their unofficial headquarters. Their penchant for drinking and barroom bragging cost them all their aircraft when Japanese spies overheard their boasts about an attack on Tsinan planned for the following day. At sunset that evening, Japanese bombers appeared over the Chinese airfield and blew apart every Vultee.

Chennault and China continued to fight the invaders, using mercenaries and whatever Chinese pilots that managed not to kill themselves in training. Their struggle wore on for more than three more years, but their fight was only delaying the inevitable. Chennault now realized that without well-trained, disciplined military pilots flying advanced aircraft there could be no victory.

By October 1940, Japanese ground forces controlled China's major port cities, and Japanese aircraft ruled its skies. China's situation grew more desperate by the day. Chiang Kai-shek summoned Chennault to Chungking (Chongqing), the generalissimo's new capital. Chiang wanted him to help procure planes and pilots in the United States. The man from Waterproof, Louisiana, responded with pessimism. He felt that U.S. neutrality and other considerations of international law would forestall any overt U.S. attempts to take sides in China's war with Japan. But Chiang would not be deterred. "You must go to the United States immediately," he said. "Work out the plans for whatever you think you need. Do what you can do to get American planes and pilots."

Chennault left at once for the United States. In Washington, D.C., he immediately encountered double forces of resistance in the persons of General Hap Arnold, who was now head of the U.S. Army Air Corps, and Rear Admiral John H. Towers, at the navy's Bureau of Aeronautics. In answer to Chennault's plea for help in procuring 100 pilots with three years of experience in fighter planes, Arnold said, "If I were to give you 100 pilots with that kind of experience, you would fold up my entire pursuit section."

Chennault, with his customary disregard for tact, snapped back, "You're wrong. If you can't spare that many pilots with that kind of experience, you don't have a pursuit section to begin with." Admiral Towers turned down the airman for the same reason. A frustrated but resolute Chennault then sought help, through influential friends, from the president of the United States.

President Franklin D. Roosevelt wanted to help, provided that a way could be found to do so without alarming the Axis powers—chiefly Germany, Italy, and Japan—with whom the United States was not yet at war. To this end, entrepreneur William Pawley and his brother Edwin formed the Central Aircraft Manufacturing Company (CAMCO). Their company would provide cover for the sale of U.S. planes to China, as well as for China's hiring of U.S. pilots. After much effort, Chennault worked out a deal to procure 100 Curtiss P-40B Tomahawk fighters—which had originally been slated for shipment to Britain—for action in China.

President Roosevelt then gave verbal orders allowing military pilots to resign their commissions, sign on with CAMCO, and fight under Chennault in China for one year. If desired, their commissions were to be reinstated at the end of their contracts. (Although it is generally believed that Roosevelt signed and issued an unofficial written order to this effect, he did not.) On the strength of Roosevelt's verbal

Birth of a Legend

orders, Chennault and his staff set off on a recruiting tour of the nation's airbases.

Visiting army, navy, and marine airbases, Chennault and his recruiters solicited volunteers with contracts offering salaries of $250 to $750 a month (depending on rank), paid housing, 30 days paid leave, and travel allowances. Added to the fringe benefits, China privately offered a $500 bonus for every Japanese plane shot down (although the CAMCO contracts made no mention of aerial combat). All together, some 240 pilots and support personnel signed up to fight for

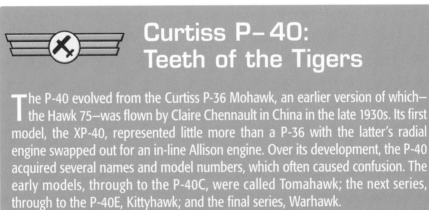

Curtiss P–40: Teeth of the Tigers

The P-40 evolved from the Curtiss P-36 Mohawk, an earlier version of which—the Hawk 75—was flown by Claire Chennault in China in the late 1930s. Its first model, the XP-40, represented little more than a P-36 with the latter's radial engine swapped out for an in-line Allison engine. Over its development, the P-40 acquired several names and model numbers, which often caused confusion. The early models, through to the P-40C, were called Tomahawk; the next series, through to the P-40E, Kittyhawk; and the final series, Warhawk.

The P-40 Tomahawks flown by the American Volunteer Group (AVG) in China were a cross between the B and C versions, that is, they were P-40Bs with some last-minute improvements added, namely, improved self-sealing fuel tanks and the addition of two more wing guns. With these enhancements, the AVG Tomahawks approximated what the army designated as P-40Cs.

In the hands of a talented pilot, the P-40 could—and did—outfight the vaunted Japanese Zero. "The P-40 had the advantage in a dive and superior firepower; whereas the Zero could climb faster, turn sharper, and cruise higher," writes AVG ace Charlie Bond. "Chennault trained us to attain higher speeds by descending on the enemy, closing in, firing, and peeling off."

Powered by a 1,000-hp Allison liquid-cooled in-line engine, the P-40C attained a top speed of 340 mph (547 kph) at 12,000 feet (3,658 meters) over a range of 700 miles (1,127 kilometers). Armed with two 50-caliber machine guns in the nose and four 7.92-mm (or .303-caliber) machine guns in the wings, the P-40 gave teeth to the Flying Tigers.

China. All volunteers, they took the name of the American Volunteer Group (AVG). They would later earn global fame and acclaim under another name.

During the summer and fall of 1941, the pilots and support personnel of the newly formed AVG, including two female nurses, set sail from San Francisco in three separate groups. They were bound for Rangoon, Burma (now called Yangon, Myanmar), via Bali, Java, Singapore, and other ports of call along the way. Their passports identified them as students, tourists, salespeople, bankers, and so on—even missionaries— so as not to draw unwanted attention their way. The conduct of some, such as that of hard-living former marine Gregory "Pappy" Boyington, tended to cast doubt on the legitimacy of the purported missionaries. Despite a few unscheduled frolics en route, the first group arrived in Rangoon in September, ready to begin training.

After a few toasts at Rangoon's Silver Grill to honor their return to dry land, the new arrivals boarded a train and jour- neyed north to the Royal Air Force (RAF) base at Toungoo. Some surprises awaited them at Kyedaw airfield, their new homebase, not the least of which was the oven-like heat, cooled only sporadically by a monsoon downpour. Bugs of a thousand varieties, or so it seemed to them, shared their wood-and-thatch living quarters, in addition to an occasional stray venomous cobra or krait. Burma, they soon learned, was something less than the romantic setting that Rudyard Kipling once immortalized in poems like *Mandalay*.

Pilot training began in the classroom with a welcoming speech by Chennault, who had arrived in Burma by air. He outlined why they were there and what he had planned for them. His training plan, he told them, consisted of 72 hours of classroom work and 60 hours of flying time. "I had been working on my plans to whip the Japanese in the air for four years," Chennault wrote in his memoirs, "and I was deter- mined that, when the American Volunteer Group went into

Gregory "Pappy" Boyington was a hard-living former marine aviator. He was just one of the former U.S. servicemen who volunteered to fight for China. Chennault had to train the pilots in his principles of air defense and early warning system.

battle, it would be using tactics based on bitter experience."

Chennault's manner, though gruff, was likable. Most AVG members would come to respect him and to feel great affection for him. Strict as he was about matters concerning training and combat, he usually made time for athletics, often joining his men for a baseball game in the evening.

During those final days before the United States entered World War II, Chennault taught his pilots well. He introduced them to his three basic principles of air defense, which he had recorded earlier in his textbook, *The Role of Defensive Pursuit*. "Successful air defense," he had written, "consists of three phases of operations: (1) detecting and reporting; (2) interception by pursuit; and (3) destruction or repulse of the invaders." And he described the workings of his early warning system, called *Jing Bao* ("to be alert") by the Chinese.

Most important, he corrected any misconceptions they might have held about inferior, nearsighted Japanese pilots. "They have been drilled for hundreds of hours," he told them, "in flying precise formations and rehearsing set tactics for each situation they may encounter." In Chennault's opinion, however, they lacked self-reliance and the ability to adapt quickly to changing conditions. AVG pilots should therefore try to break up hostile formations—both bomber and fighter— and force the enemy to improvise.

Their mentor also purged their minds of any misperceptions about the quality of Japanese aircraft. He instructed the pilots in the intricacies of the new Mitsubishi G4M1 twin-engine bomber that they would soon learn about firsthand, and in the fighting qualities of the Mitsubishi A6M—the infamous Zero. "They can turn on a dime," he cautioned, "and climb almost straight up. If they can get you in a turning combat, they are deadly."

When the volunteers finally took to the air, they immediately started practicing tactics designed by Chennault to defeat the Zero. His words no doubt echoed in their ears: "Use your speed and diving power to make a pass, shoot and break away." They worked in two-man teams to protect each other and increase their firepower (in the way of Boelcke). And they practiced, practiced, practiced—because that was Chennault's way.

Before completing their training at Toungoo, the volunteers suffered the deaths of three pilots. On September 8, John Armstrong was killed in a midair collision with fellow ex-navy pilot Gil Bright while practicing tactics. Bright parachuted to safety, but Armstrong did not. Two weeks later, ex-army pilot Maax Hammer missed the Kyedaw runway and plunged to his death. On October 25, Peter Atkinson became the second army pilot to die when a runaway propeller caused his Tomahawk to break apart during a power dive.

Low spirits among the AVG pilots received a lift when a few of them came across a photograph of a British P-40 while thumbing through an aviation magazine. A shark's face was painted on the Tomahawk's nose. Ex-army pilot Eriksen Shilling pointed out that Japanese fishermen viewed the tiger shark as a sign of bad luck, as well they might. The AVG pilots decided to adopt the fearsome symbol and painted the noses of their own P-40s to resemble tiger sharks. Unsurprisingly, the Chinese started referring to the AVG pilots as the *Fei Hou*— the "Flying Tigers"—and a legend was born.

A December to Remember

After the American Volunteer Group pilots had undergone several weeks of training, Chennault began to feel uneasy. Eighteen of his pilots, he felt, were still not ready for combat. Few of the Flying Tigers were ready for the unbelievable news that yanked them from their sleep on December 8, 1941 (December 7 in Pearl Harbor): Japanese forces were attacking American military bases in Hawaii and the Philippines.

Chennault ordered the Flying Tigers into the air at once to guard against a potential enemy surprise attack on Kyedaw airfield that might originate from Japanese bases in Thailand or Indochina (Vietnam). The results of their first "scramble" brought something less than satisfaction to their mentor. Attempting to take off in the dark without properly warming up their engines, several of Chennault's pilots lost power and nosed over into the landing strip, twisting propellers and breaking off landing gear in their eagerness to start the war. Chennault quickly called off their rush to become airborne, preferring possible damage from an enemy air strike to the self-inflicted damage of his ardent pilots. The Japanese did not attack, however, missing a chance that would cost them dearly later.

At first light, Chennault ordered a flight from one of his squadrons aloft to watch for enemy aircraft. The AVG now consisted of the First, Second, and Third Pursuit Squadrons, nicknamed *Adam and Eves* (after history's original pursuit), *Panda Bears*, and *Hell's Angels*, respectively. He ordered

The Japanese bombed the American base at Pearl Harbor, Hawaii, on December 7, 1941. Here a small boat attempts to rescue men from the USS *West Virginia*.

the rest of the AVG members to pack up and get ready to move to their new combat station at Kunming, the capital of China's Yunnan Province, about 600 miles northeast of Toungoo.

On December 12, Chennault directed the Hell's Angels, led by former army pilot Arvid E. "Oley" Olson, to join the Sixty-seventh Squadron of the RAF at Mingaladon airfield, about 10 miles north of the Burmese capital of Rangoon. "We finally worked out an agreement satisfactory to both the Generalissimo and the British, whereby one squadron of the AVG would assist the RAF in the defense of Rangoon with the other two squadrons to be stationed in Kunming," Chennault wrote later. Olson's Angels would remain under Chennault's direct command—subject only to the operational control of the RAF—which meant that the Angels could utilize Chennault's training and tactics.

The Adam and Eves and the Panda Bears, after flying over some of the roughest terrain they had ever seen— a country of mountains, gorges, jungles, and swamps— completed their move to Kunming on December 18, spoiling for a crack at the Japanese. To their dismay and anger, they found parts of the city of a half million people in smoking ruins. Earlier, Chennault had issued highly publicized orders that the two squadrons were moving to Kunming on December 17, figuring that the local Burmese would relay the news to the Japanese. He figured right. Japanese planes appeared over Kunming on the afternoon of the 17th and bombed the city, afterward claiming the destruction of 20 American aircraft. Viewing the horrors of war for the first time—maimed and charred bodies, parts of bodies, homes reduced to rubble—the Flying Tigers now wanted revenge.

Two days later, 34 P-40s stood fueled, armed, and on the alert on the 7,000-foot runway at Kunming. (After five years under construction, the runway was still being built by Chinese laborers, who crushed huge rocks and moved giant rollers by hand.) Chennault's headquarters was wired in to his early warning network, and Chinese radio operators were monitoring Japanese frequencies. At last, Chennault had all of his airmen in place and ready for a fight.

Jing Bao: Early Warning Network

Chennault's early warning network, called *Jing Bao* ("to be alert") by the Chinese, was an integral part of his air defense system. Chennault began developing the concept while commanding the Nineteenth Fighter Squadron in Hawaii in 1925. A warning network, he reasoned, would enable fighter squadrons to keep informed of the direction, height, and size of approaching enemy formations. This would allow the fighters to become airborne in sufficient time and strength to intercept and deter or destroy the enemy formations.

Chennault documented his theories on early warning in *The Role of Pursuit Aviation*, his treatise on fighter tactics, and demonstrated the network's feasibility during maneuvers held at Fort Knox in 1933. Upon his arrival in China in 1937, he set up an early warning network in the Yangtze River Valley and used it and similar networks with deadly efficiency throughout the war years.

Typically, a network consisted of concentric circles of trained spotters using the limited telephone and telegraph facilities of the region to report the approach of bombers. Plotters would chart the course of approaching aircraft on a map at a central headquarters and relay the information in time for fighter squadrons to "scramble" and for civilians to seek cover.

Chennault used a more fully developed network to protect Kunming, positioning spotters with radios at listening posts across Yunnan Province. Many spotters could only be reached by mules or by air. This "improved" network used a clock system to indicate the direction of approach, with 12 o'clock representing due north. Spotters also used codes for designating altitude and types and numbers of aircraft. A modern radar system it was not, but in China it was necessary to make do with what was available—people.

On December 20, the AVG avengers met the enemy for the first time over the town of Iliang, 30 miles southeast of Kunming. At dawn, First Pursuit Squadron leader Robert J. "Sandy" Sandell and five other Adam and Eves flew an uneventful patrol, while the rest of the first and second squadrons remained on the alert at Kunming for much of the morning. Suddenly, just as it appeared that the Japanese would not be coming, the radio crackled in Chennault's headquarters: "Ten Jap medium bombers are coming from the south; just sighted sixty miles away." Chennault scrambled his two squadrons, ordering John V. "Scarsdale Jack" Newkirk's Panda Bears to range southeast and Sandell's Adam and Eves to hang back as a rear guard in reserve.

Chennault tracked their progress by radio and chart board and waited anxiously in his air-raid dugout to hear evidence of the AVG's first contact with the enemy. "I yearned heartily to be 10 years younger," he recalled later, "crouched in a cockpit instead of a dugout, tasting the stale rubber of an oxygen mask and peering ahead into limitless space through the cherry-red rings of a gunsight."

Suddenly Jack Newkirk's voice barked across the radio waves: "Shark Fin Blue [Newkirk's radio call sign] calling base. Bandits [enemy aircraft] sighted 60 miles east. Attacking." The fight was on. And the radio went dead.

On their first diving attack on the Japanese planes—twin-engine Kawasaki Ki-48 "Lily" bombers—the Panda Bears froze in unison with "buck fever," that phenomenon of nervous excitement that momentarily paralyzes a novice hunter at the first sight of game. Their brief paralysis caused them to delay shooting for only a few seconds—long enough for the bombers to slip away.

Chennault heard the sound of bombs exploding in the distance. He figured that the Japanese must be jettisoning their bombs and fleeing in the face of Newkirk's attack. A

These Flying Tigers pose in front of a plane with the trademark tiger shark's mouth painted on the nose. The pilots enjoyed a reputation for executing daring air strikes during World War II.

few minutes later, his warning net confirmed his judgment. The bombers were heading back toward their base in Indochina. Chennault quickly ordered Sandell's Adam and Eves to take up a position over Iliang, directly in the path of the fleeing bombers.

Cruising at 16,000 feet (4,877 meters), the Adam and Eves sighted the bombers far below them at about 3,000 feet (914 meters). In their excitement, they "went a little crazy." Forgetting or ignoring all of Chennault's teachings, they sliced down on their prey and proceeded to demonstrate individual dogfighting tactics in the best tradition of World War I. They left teamwork behind in their screaming power dives to first encounters with an enemy accustomed to bombing Kunming regularly and without resistance. The ensuing action extended over a span of some 130 miles (209 kilometers). Only a miracle kept the Adam and Eves from colliding or shooting one another out of the sky.

"We opened fire, and the bombers seemed to fall to pieces," said vice squadron leader Bob Neale, summarizing the action later. "I saw pieces of engine cowling fall off into space. Glass from the gun turrets flew in all directions. Engines smoked and caught fire. Tails just crumpled and fell off. It was the queerest thing I ever saw."

When the melee ended, the Flying Tigers had shot down six bombers. Four escaped. Ed Rector, of the Panda Bears, caught up in the excitement of his first sky battle, chased one of the bombers until his P-40 ran out of gas. He crash-landed in a rice paddy with minor injuries but made it back to Kunming the next day. Rector explained that he "sure as hell wanted that one." The Japanese never again attempted to bomb Kunming while the AVG defended it.

Chennault felt elated over the AVG's first victories, but he did not want to say or do anything to promote undue cockiness in his pilots lest they become careless in their next meeting with the enemy. He gathered them together and told them, "Not a bad job, but it should have been better. Now let's go over what happened and make sure we get them all the next time." Later, he wired a message to his brother in Washington, D.C. It read: "We win the first one, six pigeons to nothing."

Contrary to a common but mistaken belief that the Flying Tigers fought for China long before America's entry into World War II, in reality, the Tigers engaged their Japanese adversaries for the first time on December 20, 1941—13 days *after* Pearl Harbor. As a final note to their first battle over Iliang, Chennault learned four years later that only *one* Japanese bomber had made it back to its base that day.

"Although the A.V.G. was blooded over China," Chennault observed later, "it was the air battles over Rangoon that stamped the hallmark on its fame as Flying Tigers." Three days after the Tigers' victory near Iliang, Olson's Hell's Angels got their first shot at the action over Burma when the Battle of Rangoon began on December 23, 1941.

The Japanese attacked the city with two waves of Mitsubishi Ki-21 heavy bombers from bases in Bangkok and Phnom Penh. The Ki-21, dubbed "Sally" by Allied pilots, was a big-tailed monoplane powered by two huge radial engines. (In World War II, the major Allies consisted of Britain, France, the Soviet Union, China, and the United States.) The Sally carried a bomb load of one metric ton.

The first wave of 18 Sallys flew unhindered over Rangoon and plastered the city's docks with high explosives. When the second wave of 20 Sallys arrived, accompanied by 20 army fighters—probably Nakajima Ki-27 "Nate" interceptors, the first Japanese monoplane fighters—20 RAF Brewster Buffalos and 16 AVG P-40s from Mingaladon airfield greeted them. And the battle began.

The Hell's Angels held to their mentor's dicta: "Fight in pairs," Chennault had told them. "Make every bullet count. Never try to get every Japanese in one pass. Hit hard, break clean, and get in position for another pass. Never worry about what's going to happen next, or it will happen to you. Keep looking around. You can lick the Japanese without getting hurt if you use your head and are careful." One by one, the Angels peeled off and attacked.

R. T. Smith, a rangy ex-army flight instructor from Nebraska, singled out a Ki-21, drew within 200 yards of it, and opened fire. "I could see my tracers converging on the fuselage and wing roots as I rapidly overtook him but kept firing until he blew up right in my face," he recalled later. "His gas tanks exploded in a huge ball of flame, the concussion tossing my plane upward like a leaf."

Charlie Older, a former navy pilot and University of California, Los Angeles, graduate, joined the battle late. He was supposed to have had the day off. He approached one of the outboard bombers from below, firing on the rise. Smoke began streaming from the bomber's port engine. "I rolled out to the side . . . and came back," Older recounted later. "I aimed again at the same plane and closed to about seventy-five yards. I gave it a long burst and the bomber suddenly nosed down out of the formation with smoke streaming behind. I saw it roll over into almost a vertical dive and disappear below."

Not everything went the Angels' way in their first fight. They lost two pilots, Neil Martin and Henry Gilbert. Martin, an ex-army pilot from Arkansas, became the AVG's first battle casualty. Attacking the bomber formation from the side, he drew fire from 27 Japanese gun turrets. His P-40 seemed to hang motionless for an instant, as if stopped in midair by the stream of cannon fire. Then it rolled over and fell to the ground. Gilbert, a native of Bremerton, Washington, and at age 21 the youngest member of the AVG, fell victim to the concentrated fire of four Nates when his P-40 went into a spin with both wings aflame.

According to a careful post-battle analysis by the RAF, the final tally at the end of the Angels' first fight showed that they had shot down 25 planes while losing two pilots and three planes. RAF pilots notched seven victories with the loss of five pilots and 11 aircraft. Despite their journeyman performance, the Angels vowed to do better the next time. They got their chance two days later—on Christmas Day.

The battle over Rangoon's Shwe Dagon pagoda on

December 25, 1941, ranks as one of history's most memorable air clashes. It began shortly after 1100 hours. The Japanese returned in force with three waves of bombers, 60 in all, and 32 fighter escorts. While the Allies were retreating in the path of seemingly unstoppable German and Japanese forces all around the globe in late December, Robert P. "Duke" Hedman, his fellow Angels, and pilots of the RAF were shattering the myth of Japanese invincibility in the skies over Rangoon on Christmas Day.

Hedman, an unassuming ex-army pilot from South Dakota, teamed up with Charlie Older and former marine pilot Thomas C. Hayward Jr. to break up the first flight of bombers. Each pilot knocked down a bomber. Five more bombers fell to AVG guns as other Angels joined the fray. Hedman then turned to meet the second wave of bombers, shooting down a Ki-27 fighter, two more bombers, and a second fighter. With five victories in one sortie, Duke Hedman became the first American ace of World War II. (A sortie is a single flight by a single plane.) And the fight went on.

The extraordinary air battle ended after an hour and a half. Many of the Angels landed almost out of gas and ammunition, their aircraft bullet-riddled and missing parts. An after-battle accounting confirmed Japanese losses at 36 aircraft, more than one-third of their attacking force. (Numerous others crashed into the sea on their return flight but were unconfirmable.) RAF pilots scored seven kills but paid for them with the loss of six of their own pilots and nine fighter planes, pretty much an even split. The Hell's Angels were officially credited with 19 kills at a cost of two P-40s. All AVG pilots returned safely.

Olson sent a radiogram report of the action to Chennault in Kunming. He received it while dining with Harvey K. Greenlaw, his executive officer, and Greenlaw's wife Olga,

The AVG and members of the RAF fought the Japanese in the skies over Burma near the Shwe Dagon pagoda in Rangoon. The Allies beat back wave after wave of Japanese bombers and fighters on Christmas Day, 1941.

to whom Chennault had assigned the role of war diary statistician. The report stated:

ALL PILOTS RETURNED AFTER BATTLE ON DECEMBER 25. SHOT DOWN TEN FIGHTERS NINE BOMBERS. LIKE SHOOTING DUCKS. WOULD PUT ENTIRE JAP FORCE OUT OF COMMISSION WITH GROUP HERE. HAVE ELEVEN PLANES LEFT. OLSON.

Grinning, Chennault shared the information with the Greenlaws and said, "The boys are going to town." Indeed, they were. Chennault's "boys" were writing a new kind of history in the skies of Asia during their first week in action. It was truly a December to remember—one that the Japanese would not soon forget.

"Without Stint or Question"

O n New Year's Day 1942, the "Old Man," as the Flying Tigers affectionately referred to Chennault, sent Scarsdale Jack Newkirk's Panda Bears to Rangoon to relieve some of Oley Olson's Hell's Angels. By the end of January, Chennault would completely replace the Angels with Sandy Sandell's more rested Adam and Eves.

Newkirk, known for his aggressive leadership, wasted no time joining the action. Two days after his squadron's arrival at Mingaladon airfield, he led an offensive reconnaissance of Japanese airfields in Thailand. David Lee "Tex" Hill, an ex-navy bomber pilot, and James H. Howard, who had flown fighter planes off the carrier *Enterprise*, accompanied Newkirk. Jack's wingman, Bert Christman, an ex-navy pilot and former comic-strip artist in civilian life, started out with the flight but dropped out when a balky engine forced him to return to base.

The wingman's job was to defend the flight leader, his partner in Chennault's two-man team, shifting from left to right, then back again, always covering the leader's flanks and rear. This coverage enabled the flight leader to press in for the kill with his tail protected.

The three Pandas flew east across the iridescent waters of Martaban Bay to attack the enemy airfield at Tak (Rahaeng). They arrived at Tak just as a half-dozen Japanese Nakajima Ki-27 fighters, called Nates, were landing after a raid on the RAF airbase at Moulmein, three touching down and three still

Chennault posed at the Kunming air base in front of one of his squadron's planes. He had planned to visit his men in Rangoon, but a bout with influenza kept him grounded in China.

in the air. The Pandas saw only the three on the ground. Mistakenly believing the Ki-27s to be taking off, they attacked.

"I got so preoccupied with seeing the enemy planes on the ground," Tex Hill recalled years later, "that I didn't think about looking up. The three of us bent 'em [their P-40s] over, and as we approached the field I looked up *and there were three more planes in the traffic pattern with us.* Like lightning, one Jap tacked on to Jim Howard's tail and was eating him up." Hill quit his own strafing run and attacked the Nate on his endangered friend's tail. Newkirk would have to deal with the other two Nates.

"I pulled around on him as quickly as I could and started firing as I did," Hill said later. "I didn't even look through the gunsights — just watched the tracers like following a garden hose. With my diving speed built up, I came right up on him and he blew up. I flew through the debris and pulled up to come around and meet another Jap coming right at me." Hill thought that he had also shot down the second Nate but Newkirk claimed it.

Newkirk locked on to the Nate's tail only to see it loop up and away, then swing around and head straight back at him. "Both of us were firing head on at each other," Newkirk reported later, "and he pulled up over me. Several particles fell from his plane and he stalled and spun into the jungle."

All three Panda Bears made it back to Mingaladon. Howard received credit for destroying four Nates on the ground. Newkirk was credited with two kills in the air and Hill one.

On January 9, Newkirk led a similar raid against the Tak airfield with four Panda Bears — Noel Bacon, Pete Wright, Percy Bartelt, and Tex Hill — and six RAF pilots. "We dived from ten thousand feet and caught 'em flatfooted, working on their planes," Newkirk reported afterward. "We blasted three planes and three trucks to smithereens on the very first run. Then we went back and really got going." The final results showed that the AVG/RAF raid on Tak destroyed 24 Japanese planes and three trucks on the ground and hit most of the buildings with machine-gun bullets.

Newkirk, excited over the performance of his Panda Bears, radioed Chennault: "The more hardships, work, and fighting that the men have to do, the higher the morale goes. They seem to thrive on adversity." But losses, accidents, and illnesses had thinned the ranks of the Pandas to the extent that Newkirk could only put 10 aircraft into service.

Chennault sent eight of Sandell's Tomahawks down from Kunming on January 12. On that same day, Lieutenant General Shojiro Iida's Imperial Japanese Fifteenth Army began its westward push into Burma from Thailand. Between January 23 and 27, the Japanese mounted six major attacks on the AVG.

On the first day of the new aerial onslaught, three Nates attacked Bert Christman, the comic-strip artist, at 12,000 feet (3,658 meters) and knocked out his Allison in-line engine. Christman bailed out. One of the Nates swung around and machine-gunned him to death in his parachute. Ed Rector chased Christman's killer downward, pouring fire into the Nate and forcing the pilot to bail out at about 300 feet (91 meters). His parachute opened too late, just as he hit the ground.

Chennault had hoped to visit his squadrons in Rangoon, but a bout of influenza, coupled with his chronic bronchitis, debilitated him for most of the winter. "I alternated between brief spells in my airfield office," he wrote of his sick period, "and longer sieges in my sick bed." But from his sick bed, he monitored the activities of his Flying Tigers by radio and controlled their operations. To help defend against the new Japanese attacks, he sent the rest of the Adam and Eves to Rangoon on January 25.

Former marine Greg Boyington, who had griped that the First Pursuit Squadron "might just as well been back in the United States blowing bubbles in the bathtub," was finally

The American fighters, including Gregory Boyington (shown here), piloted P-40 Tomahawks. They were forced to improvise during battles to keep the advantage against the more maneuverable Ki-27 Nates used by the Japanese.

going to grab a slice of the action. During his first hostile encounter, he nearly fell victim to new Japanese tactics.

To use the P-40's superior diving speed to best advantage, the AVG pilots usually attacked from above, swooping down and cutting their targets out of an enemy formation. The new Japanese tactics called for pilots to open their formation as the Tigers dived on them, allowing the Flying P-40s to pass through without scoring. Then, as the AVG aircraft struggled to regain altitude, the Japanese pilots would flip their nimble fighters over into tight half-loops—a maneuver known to pilots as a split-S maneuver—and plummet upon the disadvantaged P-40s.

Boyington's flight of 10 P-40s, rising to meet 40 to 50 Ki-27 Nates in a hazy sky, found itself facing a similar disadvantage. Louis "Cokey" Hoffman, the oldest member of the AVG at 43, was flying wingman for Bob Prescott, when several of the Nates flipped over into split-Ss and dropped down on him, spouting flame in his direction. Boyington later described Cokey's P-40 as giving "all the appearance of a fish writhing in agony out of water." The Tomahawk spun to the ground, killing Hoffman.

Boyington twice got caught in turning situations with the tighter-turning Nates but finally dived for safety and escaped. A quick learner, Greg shot down two Nates in his next outing, during a tiff in which the Flying Tigers shot down a total of 16 Japanese planes. Sandy Sandell shot down three Nates to become the first ace of the Adam and Eves. After notching two victories, Boyington felt excited on his flight back to Mingaladon, but he would not let himself become too enthusiastic. As he wrote later, he now "knew only too well that this was going to be a struggle for survival—not for money."

On January 30, two Panda Bears were ordered to attack the enemy airbase at Tak and the Japanese ground troops advancing on Moulmein. George Burgard, one of these pilots, called it a "stupid" mission, saying "our ships are so few, and our pilots so valuable, it is complete nonsense to use them for such senseless missions." Tommy Cole, who volunteered to fly along on the strafing run, went down from ground fire in a ball of flame.

Four days later, Chennault recalled the Panda Bears to Kunming. "[T]hey were down to 10 P-40s," he explained later, "so I sent Bob Sandell and his First Squadron to take up the burden at Rangoon. The Japanese ground offensive into Burma had begun to roll during the last weeks in January, and it was evident that the British had neither the men, equipment, nor leadership to stop it." The Adam and Eves could only hope to delay the inevitable. But they would have to do it without Sandell.

On February 7, Sandell was killed in a crash at Mingaladon while flight testing his P-40 after it had undergone repairs. Chennault appointed vice squadron leader Bob Neale to succeed Sandy. Neale, an ex-navy pilot from Seattle, faced the formidable task of leading the Adam and Eves in the final phase of the air battle over Rangoon. He would have plenty of enemies to engage.

Following the fall of Singapore in mid-February, the Japanese shifted the crack air units that blasted the RAF from the skies above Malaya and Singapore to Thailand to join the assault on Rangoon. These additions—including the Zero fighter—boosted the enemy air strength to some 400 planes for its drive on Rangoon. Moving toward the end of February, the Japanese struck at the city with 200 planes a day. And the end drew near.

Neale radioed Chennault for evacuation instructions. Chennault replied: "Expend equipment. Conserve personnel utmost. Leave with last oxygen bottle." The new squadron leader took the Old Man's orders literally, awaiting the final Japanese push with nine P-40s.

On February 25, the Adam and Eves and a handful of RAF Hurricanes—the Hawker fighter plane that had teamed with the Supermarine Spitfire to win the Battle of Britain in the summer of 1940—fought off 166 Japanese planes in three raids. Neale's pilots, now down to 6 P-40s, bagged 24 of them.

It got worse the next day when 200 more Japanese planes darkened the skies over Rangoon. Again, Neale's pilots met the challenge. They notched 18 more victories to up their total to 42 in two days. On the February 28, Neale, down to his last bottle of oxygen, ordered his pilots back to the RAF base at Magwe, about 200 miles north of Rangoon. "In those two days of almost constant air fighting," Chennault wrote in his memoirs, "Neale's detachment turned in one of the epic fighter performances of all time."

Another qualified judge of fine air fighting also praised their accomplishments. "The magnificent victories these Americans have won over the paddy fields of Burma are

The Zero Fighter

The Mitsubishi A6M Zero-Sen (Type 0 Fighter) was unquestionably the most famous and most used Japanese fighter plane of World War II. It first saw combat over China in 1940 and remained in first-line service until the very end of the war.

In the fall of 1940, Claire Chennault forwarded a report to Washington with a photograph of the Zero and estimates of its performance. He warned that disaster would befall any American or British fighter plane attempting to dogfight with the new Japanese aircraft. The U.S. War Department replied: "Bunk. Such an airplane is an aerodynamic impossibility." In the best judgment of War Department officials, Japan was incapable of designing and manufacturing such a high-performance aircraft. They could not have been more wrong. Their lack of vision enabled the Japanese to keep the secret of the Zero until their shocking attacks on Pearl Harbor and the Philippines in December 1941.

The Zero—code-named "Zeke" by the Allies—had a maximum speed of 316 mph (509 kph), a service ceiling of 33,790 feet (10,299 meters), and a range of 1,940 miles (3,122 kilometers). Its light construction and lack of self-sealing fuel tanks and armor plating to protect the pilot gave the Zero its phenomenal maneuverability and range. Early versions were armed with a 20-mm cannon and a 7.7-mm machine gun in each wing, later versions, in addition to the cannon, carried a 13.2-mm machine gun in each wing and one in the fuselage. The Zero was also fitted with underwing launch rails capable of carrying eight 132-pound (60-kilogram) bombs or two air-to-air rockets.

A versatile aircraft, the Zero was used as a fighter, a fighter-bomber, and, fitted with floats, an observation plane launched from warships. Early versions were used in great numbers in *kamikaze* — suicide-bombing — attacks in the waning months of the war.

comparable in character if not in scope with those won by the Royal Air Force over the orchards and hop fields of Kent in the Battle of Britain," said Winston Churchill, Britain's indomitable prime minister.

Despite the gallant AVG and RAF defense of Rangoon, the Burmese capital fell to the Japanese invaders on March 7, 1942. Chennault then turned his attention to the defense of the Burma Road, the winding supply route chiseled out of mountainsides from Lashio to Kunming by thousands of Chinese laborers. The Burma Road, 320 miles (515 kilometers) of straight road and 717 miles (1,154 kilomteters) of one hairpin turn after another, represented Chennault's—and China's—only overland link with the outside world.

The nature of battle changed as British and U.S. troops— the Americans under the command of Lieutenant General Joseph W. "Vinegar Joe" Stilwell—fought a slow withdrawal action in Burma. Air-to-air action became catch-as-catch-can. Chiang Kai-shek called on Chennault to use his Flying Tigers in close support of ground troops. The Tigers, most of whom considered themselves more valuable as aerial defenders, were now forced to embark—albeit reluctantly—on a prolonged campaign of bombing and strafing runs.

Three weeks into March 1942, the Japanese began attacking Magwe. They were now attacking the American Volunteer Group only when they could catch U.S. planes on the ground. On March 21, over the course of 24 hours, a force of 266 Japanese bombers and fighters—including G4M Sallys and A6M Zeros— all but obliterated the RAF airbase at Magwe. The Adam and Eves left Magwe for a brief stay at Loiwing, Burma. After being relieved by the Hell's Angels, Neale and his bunch went home to Kunming. By then, they had accumulated 44 air victories.

On March 23, Chennault ordered retaliatory raids against Japanese airbases at Lampang and Chiengmai (Chiang Mai) in Thailand. The raids were successful but costly. Antiaircraft fire claimed William "Black Mac" McGarry's P-40, forcing him to bail out. He spent most of the rest of the war in a Bangkok jail, interned by the Thai government. Scarsdale Jack Newkirk was less fortunate. Struck by ground fire, he crashed in a ball of flame and was killed instantly.

The new low-level sorties in support of Chinese troops, forced on Chennault's pilots by Chiang Kai-shek and Stilwell, began to wear on the Flying Tigers. Their spirits dropped. Stilwell's increased demands for stricter military discipline rankled them further. Fresh supplies and new equipment failed to arrive as promised. Their spirits hit the subbasement level when Stilwell ordered additional low-level reconnaissance missions. This was dangerous work because it put the pilots at the mercy of Japanese aircraft attacking from above and out of the sun. The Tigers began to rebel.

On April 15, 1942, the army reinstated Chennault as a brigadier general in the U.S. Army Air Force. His men remained civilians under contract to the Central Aircraft Manufacturing Company (CAMCO). The army ordered him to start preparing to merge the Flying Tigers into an air force unit. Not many Tigers favored the merger. The prospect of becoming assimilated by the air force was especially appalling to the former navy and marine pilots. Pappy Boyington, who went on to become a top-ranking marine ace in the South Pacific, was the first Tiger to quit. His resignation set the tone for others to follow.

When informed of another low-level bombing attack on the Japanese airfield at Chiengmai, in which they would fly escort to British Blenheim bombers, the Tigers threatened to quit en masse. Only a moving speech by Tex Hill, the number two ace of the Tigers, headed off a mutiny:

> We came to China as mercenaries, there are no bones about that, but we now have a different situation. Our country is at war. And these are our orders. This is what the Old Man says we got to do. We ought to do it.

The mission was scheduled for April 19. Tex went on to stress its importance and volunteered to lead it. His offer became unnecessary, however, as the Blenheim bombers failed to show up and the mission was canceled. But the mood of discontent lingered, and the end of the American Volunteer Group came into view.

On April 29, in the face of Japanese advances to Lashio, the Tigers evacuated Loiwing and returned to Kunming. Another Flying Tiger fell from the ranks of the AVG on May 4, when shrapnel from a Japanese bomb struck Benny Foshee on the ground at an AVG auxiliary airfield at Paoshan. Foshee died from blood loss before his friends could get him to a doctor.

The first battle for Burma ended on May 11. In 10 weeks of fighting, AVG pilots, with only between 5 and 20 aircraft available to them on any given day, met 31 separate Japanese attacks in the skies over Asia. The enemy's forces often numbered more than 100 planes. The Tigers bagged 217 hostile aircraft and logged 43 probables, while losing 16 P-40s and seven pilots. By comparison, RAF pilots recorded 74 victories, 33 probables, and lost 22 planes during that same time frame. Clearly, the Old Man's training and tactics had paid off.

The next day another Tiger fell. John Donovan died in a fiery explosion when antiaircraft fire tore a gaping hole in his P-40 during a raid on the Japanese airbase at Gia Lam in Hanoi. On May 22, Bob Little answered destiny's call during a bombing mission over the Salween Gorge. One of the wings of his new P-40E Kittyhawk disintegrated, probably when a lucky hit from small-arms ground fire detonated a bomb in his wing rack. His plane was aflame when it hit the ground and exploded. Little was the last of the AVG pilots to die in combat.

With American forces back in China, General Stilwell,

Joseph Stilwell was Chiang Kai-shek's chief of staff and commander of the U.S. armed forces in China. Stilwell and Chennault had a long-running disagreement about the use of air power to defeat Japan.

now Chiang Kai-shek's chief of staff and commander of American forces in China, became personally involved in directing Flying Tiger operations, progressively demanding more and more of them. Stilwell's direct involvement with the Tigers pleased neither Chennault nor his pilots. Hard feelings quickly developed between the aviator Chennault and the foot soldier Stilwell. And when junior and senior officers disagree, the subordinate officer rarely if ever wins the argument. Chennault's problems with the dissenting views of the military power structure began all over again.

More and more, Chennault found his authority limited by the politics of high command. Chennault's powers deteriorated further yet when Clayton Bissell, his old nemesis from the Air Corps Tactical School, arrived in China to assume command of the newly formed Tenth Air Force—a position that Chennault had wanted. Plans for merging the Tigers into the air force shifted into high gear now, as the contracts of many of them were due to expire shortly.

On July 4, 1942, the American Volunteer Group was officially disbanded. Their accomplishments in six-plus months of air fighting defy superlatives. General Chennault, with great satisfaction, summed up the record of the AVG this way:

> The group that the military experts predicted would not last three weeks in combat had fought for seven months over Burma, China, Thailand, and French Indo-China, destroying 299 Japanese planes with another 153 probably destroyed. All of this with a loss of 12 P–40s in combat and 61 on the ground, including the 22 burned at Loi-Wing. Four pilots were killed in the air combat; six were killed by antiaircraft fire; three by enemy bombers on the ground; and three were taken prisoner. Ten more died as a result of flying accidents.

In more than 50 air battles with the Japanese, the AVG pilots never lost a fight. On their final day before slipping away into history, the Flying Tigers shot down six Ki-27 Nate fighters over Hengyang.

Of the AVG, Chennault later recalled, "[W]hen there was a fight to be fought and an objective to be gained, they gave all they had, without stint or question." The record shows that the same might be said of their leader.

The Fourteenth
Air Force

At one minute after midnight on July 5, the Twenty-third
Fighter Group of the Tenth Air Force was formed to replace
the American Volunteer Group. The pilot roster of the new
fighter group included the names of only five Flying Tigers—
Gil Bright, Tex Hill, Ed Rector, Charlie Sawyer, and Frank
Schiel. Sixteen Tigers signed on with the China National Aviation
Corporation and remained in Asia to fly desperately needed
supplies and matériel from India to China. Dick Rossi, an AVG
ace with 6.29 victories flew across the dangerous Himalayas—the
"Hump"—735 times. Most of those who went back to the United
States reenlisted in their former services.

Chennault's service to China and to his own country did not
end with the breakup of the AVG. A new season of warfare began
for him, and for the five Tigers who chose to stay with him when
he assumed command of the China Air Task Force (CATF). The

CATF comprised the Twenty-third Fighter Group and the Eleventh Bombardment Group.

Chennault later recalled that the CATF "was patched together in the midst of combat from whatever happened to be available in China during the gloomy summer of 1942." Although it formed a part of the army's Tenth Air Force, which was headquartered in far-off Delhi, India, the CATF enjoyed little more than second-rate status. Chennault had to battle for every pilot, plane, bullet, bomb, and drop of gasoline. But he did whatever it took to continue the fight

(From left to right): British Allied commander John Dill and U.S. commanders Claire Chennault, Henry Arnold, Joseph Stilwell, and Clayton Bissell stroll past an AVG fighter plane.

against Japan, including shuttling men and airplanes from base to base on a 5,000-mile (8,046-kilometer) front.

The airfield at Kweilin served as his center of operations. Other operational bases included Hengyang and Lingling. Despite perpetual shortages of everything needed to fight an air war, he continually sent his men against the enemy at locations ranging from Burma to Indochina to eastern China. Again, he waged war with minimal resources.

The Twenty-third Fighter Group, commanded by Colonel Robert L. Scott (who later achieved renown as the author of *God Is My Co-Pilot*), and the Eleventh Bombardment Group, led by Colonel Caleb V. Haynes, waged a ragtag war until the spring of 1943. The Twenty-third continued in the tradition of the Flying Tigers, shooting down 149 Japanese aircraft—not counting another 85 probable kills—at the cost of 16 P-40s. At the same time, the Eleventh dropped more than 300 tons of bombs on Japanese targets, with the loss of only one B-25.

During this same period, Chennault continued to struggle with the military power structure over conflicting views and policy decisions. He developed a plan for defeating the enemy through the use of air power. And he strove to become the top U.S. commander in China in order to implement his plan. But his superiors—Bissell and Stilwell again—still opposed his views and fought him in every way possible. Chennault again sought the help of President Franklin D. Roosevelt.

In a letter to Wendell Wilkie, the defeated Republican candidate for president in 1942, who was then acting as Roosevelt's personal envoy on an around-the-world inspection tour, Chennault outlined a plan for victory through air power. "Japan can be defeated in China," he declared. "It can be defeated by an Air Force so small that in other theaters it would be called ridiculous."

He explained his reasons for believing in victory through air power in great detail. Given such a force, he wrote, and full authority as American commander in China, he could cause the collapse of Japan, thereby saving hundreds of thousands of American lives, and at a small cost. He argued with his usual disregard for tact that the military task in China was a simple one made complex by an unwieldy, illogical military organization and by men who lacked understanding of aerial warfare in China. To accomplish all this, he would need only 105 fighter aircraft of advanced design, 30 medium bombers, and 12 heavy bombers, all subject to constant maintenance and continual replacement.

He noted that it was "essential" that he "be given complete freedom of fighting action" and also be empowered "to deal directly with the Generalissimo and the Chinese forces." That such an arrangement would, at best, subjugate the role of Stilwell, his present superior, he left unsaid. He predicted that his strategy would assure successful operations by Chinese ground forces and enable the success of army advances and naval operations in the Pacific. In closing, Chennault added, "Moreover, it will make China our lasting friend for years after the war."

Wilkie delivered the letter to President Roosevelt upon his return to Washington, where it caused a big stir in the War Department. Army chief of staff General George C. Marshall, though no admirer of Chennault, felt compelled to admit that the maverick airman from Louisiana was quite likely "a tactical genius." But Chennault's brash attempt to replace Stilwell, who enjoyed favored status with the army chief, infuriated Marshall. He impugned Chennault's plan, characterizing it as "just nonsense; not bad strategy, just nonsense," and supported Stilwell's alternative plan for winning the war on the ground.

In Roosevelt's judgment, however, Chennault's plan offered appealing advantages over Stilwell's concept of ground warfare in the near-impassable jungle and mountainous terrain of Asia, and its inherent promise of a long, drawn-out conflict.

Chennault's way held a distinct cost-savings advantage, both in money and in lives, and it provided an avenue for Chiang Kai-shek's China to become the major power in Asia by filling the void left by Japan at war's end. Notwithstanding Marshall's support for his friend Stilwell, and despite the War Department's extreme displeasure with the brazen airpower advocate, the power of the presidency lent full sway to Chennault's plan.

On March 10, 1943, President Roosevelt dissolved the

"Vinegar Joe" Stilwell

General Joseph W. Stilwell, West Point graduate and veteran of both world wars, saw more frontline combat in World War II than any other American four-star general.

At the U.S. Military Academy, he graduated 32nd in a class of 124 in 1904. In his early career before World War I, he served twice in the Philippines. He fought guerrillas on Samar in 1904 during his first tour of duty in the islands. In 1911, while on leave during his second tour in the Philippines, he visited China, which was then embroiled in a revolution. Stilwell served as an intelligence officer with General John J. "Black Jack" Pershing's American Expeditionary Force in France in 1918 and helped to plan the St. Mihiel offensive.

After World War I, Stilwell served three tours of duty in China between 1920 and 1939. His understanding of Chinese culture and society gained during these assignments led to his appointment as senior U.S. commander in Asia during World War II. He headed several commands in the China-Burma-India theater of operations. During the collapse of Allied forces in Burma in 1942, he led his headquarters group on a march through treacherous jungles and across high mountains to Imphal, India.

Stilwell's irascibility earned him the nickname of "Vinegar Joe." Despite his outstanding military performance, his lack of tact and differing policy views with Chiang Kai-shek led to his recall from China at Chiang's request in October 1944. Whatever he lacked in diplomacy he made up for in able and vigorous military leadership. As one of his associates phrased it, he was "sarcastic but in a way that made you want to perform. I would have done anything for him."

China Air Task Force and created the China-based Fourteenth Air Force with Chennault at its head. As commander of the Fourteenth Air Force in China, Chennault finally managed to move himself out from under the control of his old adversary Clayton Bissell. Given the second star of a major general, Chennault was subordinate to only Lieutenant General Stilwell in China, but only marginally so. At last, Chennault believed, he could assemble a "real" air force.

Chennault started out small with the men and machines of the CATF, gradually building up his forces with the arrival of newer, faster fighter planes—North American P-51C Mustangs—and larger, four-engine bombers—Consolidated B-24 Liberators. He watched his air force grow from 100 aircraft and 250 men to 1,000 aircraft and 20,000 men. Chennault used them well.

Chennault now felt totally convinced that the war against Japan could be won through airpower. Stilwell felt just as strongly that the war must be won on the ground, believing that Chennault's airfields could be too easily over-run by Japanese ground troops. Stilwell favored building up Chinese ground forces until they were strong enough to regain the land lost to the enemy, starting with recapturing Burma. Even Britain's prime minister Winston Churchill frowned on Stilwell's battle plan, however, likening the recapture of Burma to "munching a porcupine, quill by quill." On the other hand, Chiang Kai-shek fully endorsed Chennault's strategy.

Toward the end of April 1943, Roosevelt, at Chiang Kai-shek's request, called Chennault back for strategy sessions in Washington. General Marshall—still incensed with what he perceived as Chennault's end run and blatant attempt to usurp his friend's command—arranged for Stilwell's return as well. The president's perception of the two warriors and their contrasting demeanors played a large part in what happened next.

Generalissimo Chiang Kai-shek, President Franklin D. Roosevelt, and Prime Minister Winston Churchill met in November 1943 in Cairo, Egypt, to discuss their goals regarding Japan. The leaders confirmed their plan to pursue the war until Japan surrendered.

Each general had a private conference with Roosevelt. Chennault exuded confidence, assuring the president that his planes could sink millions of tons of Japanese shipping. By contrast, Stilwell, discomforted by having to justify his strategic posture to the president, appeared halting and nearly tongue-tied in Roosevelt's eyes. According to Marshall, Stilwell sat slumped over with his head down and "muttered something about China not fighting." Stilwell wanted Chiang to commit all available Chinese forces to the ground war. Chiang figured that Chennault's way was quicker and less costly to China.

Later, when both generals appeared at the Trident Conference, which was held from May 11 to 25, 1943, in Washington—an Allied strategy session convened by no less a figure than Churchill himself—two fine patriots with honest differences met to champion the case for their deepest beliefs. One of them had to lose.

Stilwell argued for a ground offensive. He pointed out that without well-trained Chinese ground forces to prevent the Japanese from capturing Chennault's vulnerable airfields there could be no air offensive, an argument that bore great merit. His opponents argued that the means for launching a ground offensive in Asia were not then available. Instead, they opted to limit ground activities to those essential to support an air offensive.

On another level, Chennault's enthusiasm and salesmanship carried the day over Vinegar Joe Stilwell's sullen and often ill-tempered demeanor. To the bitter disappointment of Stilwell, Chennault left Washington with logistical (supply) priorities assigned to the Fourteenth Air Force and orders to proceed with his air offensive against Japan.

Stilwell, old soldier that he was, returned to China to carry out his new orders to the best of his ability. His diary entry on the return flight reflected his unhappiness. "What's the use when the World's Greatest Strategist [Chennault] is against you?" he asked himself. Stilwell left China and his harried command in October 1944, replaced by Major General Albert C. Wedemeyer. Vinegar Joe had done his best.

Chennault, although disappointed that Roosevelt passed him over for supreme command in China, remained to fight on. Chennault's offensive began in June 1943, and with it the summing up and testing out of all the ideas on warfare that he had developed over the years. This offensive included what came to be known as "Project Matterhorn," the bombing of the Japanese home islands by Boeing B-29 Superfortresses flying from bases in China.

Under Chennault, the Fourteenth Air Force compiled a record that would please any battlefield commander, destroying more than 2,600 Japanese planes, with another 1,500 probables listed, while losing some 500 aircraft of its own. In other actions, its bombers sank 44 ships, knocked out 600 bridges, and wiped out nearly 67,000 enemy troops. But the end of Chennault's tenure as its head came into view in the spring of 1945.

Following the death of President Roosevelt in April 1945— which left Chennault without friends in high places—Hap Arnold, Chennault's old detractor, started pressing for his retirement. Arnold wanted to replace the Fourteenth Air Force with the Tenth, then commanded by Major General George Stratemeyer. Chennault saw what the future held and sent a letter to General Wedemeyer requesting retirement.

Wedemeyer granted Chennault's request and at the same time awarded him the Distinguished Service Cross for being "a major factor in rendering impotent the enemy's air drive in China" while reflecting "great honor upon himself and the military service." Later, Generalissimo Chiang Kai-shek hosted a farewell dinner for Chennault, highlighting the evening by presenting him with the White Sun and Blue Sky medallion, China's highest award. It is doubtful that any warrior ever deserved the honors more.

Sick at heart, Chennault left China on August 8, 1945, less than a month before the official end of the war. Convinced that he had not been treated fairly, he later wrote to a friend, "I wanted to see it through, but not on the terms offered me." The war ended after U.S. B-29s dropped atomic bombs on Hiroshima and Nagasaki on August 6 and 9, respectively. Japan formally surrendered on September 2, 1945.

After the war, Lieutenant General Takahashi, commander of the Japanese forces in central China, wrote that had it not been for the Fourteenth Air Force, "we could have gone anywhere we wished" in China.

Twenty-five days after Chennault's departure from China, General Douglas MacArthur formally accepted Japan's surrender aboard the U.S. battleship *Missouri* in Tokyo Bay. After signing two copies of the surrender document—one in English, the other in Japanese—MacArthur surveyed the innumerable faces of the witnesses present. Turning to his aide, he asked, "Where's Chennault?"

Such Things
As Others
Only Dream Of

Returning home after long years of separation from his wife, Chennault found that the love he once shared with Nell had faded. They soon agreed to dissolve their marriage and parted friends. The old warhorse retired from the army for a second time on October 31, 1945. After only five months, Chennault returned to China—and to a new love, Anna Chan, a 20-year-old reporter who had once interviewed him. He arrived in Shanghai on New Year's Day 1946 and set out on a three-week trek through the war-ravaged land that he had come to love.

Traveling inland, Chennault observed firsthand the ruins left behind by the war, the starving people, the devastation, and the misery that was China. "Families yoked themselves in [water] buffalo harness, and tried to drag heavy wooden plows and harrows through thick rice-paddy mud," he reported, "but their half-starved bodies were unequal to the task." Railways had been cut and bridges bombed out, while food and other vital supplies were piling up on the docks of China's ports. Chennault met with the Chiangs and other Chinese leaders. A new air transport service was needed, he told them, to move essential supplies across the vast reaches of China. They all agreed.

Once again China's leaders called upon Chennault to form an air service. And once again Chennault answered their call, this time by forming the Civil Air Transport (CAT), whose acronym suggests to some a symbolic connection to the past. Chennault's business manager and partner Whiting Willaeur, for example, noted, "CAT comes pretty close to spelling Tiger." But this was a different breed of cat.

In May 1946, Chennault returned to the United States to seek financing for his new air service. With the help of former New

Chennault returned to China in 1946, arriving in Shanghai on New Year's Day. The city in eastern China had been taken over by Japan in 1937 and occupied until the end of the war in 1945.

York City mayor Fiorello La Guardia, who was now director of the United Nations Relief and Rehabilitation Agency, Chennault arranged a loan and bought 19 surplus Curtiss C-46 Commandos and Douglas C-47 Skytrains. Chennault and Willaeur recruited a group of ex-military personnel to maintain and fly them, including former American Volunteer Group pilots Joe Rosbert and Erik Shilling. The CAT took to the air on January 31, 1947, flying the first relief cargo west from Canton (Guangzhou). As Chennault noted later, it flew "under the sign of a new and more docile Flying Tiger."

At the same time, another group of former AVG pilots—headed by Bob Prescott and including Bill Bartling, Duke Hedman, Robert "Catfish" Raines, Dick Rossi, and other Flying Tigers—were forming an airline in the United States. It eventually bore the name of the Flying Tiger Line. Rossi flew as a captain with the freight line for about 25 years, logging a lifetime of more than 25,000 flying hours.

On December 21, 1947, Claire Chennault and Anna Chan exchanged marriage vows in a simple wedding at the general's house in Shanghai. Anna, the well-educated, petite, and alluring daughter of the Chinese consul to San Francisco, became Chennault's adoring and devoted companion for the rest of his life.

By April 1948, Chennault's air service was operating successfully, hauling tons of materials a month and helping to lift China back on its feet. By then, the civil war in China between the Nationalists of Chiang Kai-shek and the Communists of Mao Tse-tung (Mao Ze-dong), which Chiang had anticipated for years, had erupted and was in full swing. Chennault regretted that "some Chinese people are in open rebellion against their government—thereby delaying the rehabilitation of their country and diminishing its prestige as a world power." At first, however, he did not "feel it is my duty to participate in this needless, bitter conflict. My desire is to aid all Chinese." But as the civil war wore on, Chennault became increasingly anti-Communist.

Chennault became more and more convinced that the spread of Communism in Southeast Asia posed a threat to the United States and to the Free World. He and Willaeur decided to cast their lot with Chiang Kai-shek's Nationalists and to use the CAT to support his forces. With regard to China's ongoing civil war, Chennault figured that his old friend Chiang possessed "both the desire and the power to clear the situation rapidly." But he misjudged Chiang's military capabilities.

During the Communist siege of Mukden, Manchuria, the

AVG Aces

From December 20, 1941, through July 4, 1942, twenty-six pilots from the American Volunteer Group shot down five or more enemy planes to qualify as aces:

Name	Victories	Name	Victories
Percy Bartelt	7.00	William McGarry	10.29
W. E. Bartling	7.27	Bob Neale	15.55
Lew Bishop	5.20	Jack Newkirk	10.50
Charlie Bond	8.77	Charlie Older	10.08
Gil Bright	6.00	Ed Overend	5.83
George Burgard	10.79	Bob Prescott	5.29
Thomas Haywood	5.08	Ed Rector	6.52
Tex Hill	11.25	Bill Reed	10.50
Jim Howard	6.33	Dick Rossi	6.29
Ken Jernstedt	10.50	Bob Sandell	5.27
Chauncey Laughlin	5.20	Frank Schiel	7.00
Frank Lawlor	8.50	Robert H. Smith	5.50
Robert Little	10.55	R. T. Smith	8.73

* As compiled by Daniel Ford in Flying Tigers, pp. 387-88.

In 1948, Chennault's Civil Air Transport (CAT) carried Chinese Nationalist soldiers to and from areas torn apart by China's civil war.

CAT airlifted in thousands of tons of food, medicine, and other essential supplies. On return trips, CAT pilots and planes ferried out noncombatants and wounded soldiers. But Mukden became a death trap for entire Nationalist armies, flown in and supplied by CAT. At one point, Chennault's crews flew as many as 50 missions a day, braving artillery fire and landing on hastily built airfields to sustain Chiang's armies. But Mukden fell to the Communists, as did Manchuria and northern China.

Thereafter, the Communists forced the Nationalists to withdraw first to Canton and finally to Taiwan. Chennault and the CAT moved with the Nationalists to Taiwan in October 1949—but not before losing, for all practical purposes, 73 of his airplanes to the Communists. Despite its losses and a subsequent battle with insolvency, Chennault's CAT weathered the squalls of adversity and continued to operate but only on a shoestring—nothing new to Chennault.

When war broke out in Korea in 1950, the U.S. Central Intelligence Agency (CIA) acquired the Civil Air Transport from Chennault, Willaeur, and other stockholders. The CIA used CAT planes to fly troops and supplies in support of the United Nations. And when French troops were surrounded by Communist forces at Dien Bien Phu in French Indochina (Vietnam) in 1954, CAT pilots in Fairchild C-119 Flying Boxcars flew many flights to parachute urgently needed supplies to the beleaguered French soldiers.

On one relief flight into Dien Bien Phu, pilot James McGovern—nicknamed "Earthquake McGoon" after Al Capp's lovable villain in the comic strip Li'l Abner—and his copilot Wallace Buford, were attempting to airdrop six tons of ammunition when a shell from a Soviet-built 37-mm gun knocked out one of the engines of their twin-engine Boxcar. It began losing altitude rapidly.

Another shell tore into one of the Boxcar's twin booms that supported the plane's tail surfaces. Buford and a crew of French cargo handlers stayed with the crippled aircraft while McGovern tried to coax it beyond the encircled French fortifications lest its cargo detonate among the besieged troops below. "It looks like this is it," McGovern was heard to say to Buford over an open microphone. An instant later, the cargo plane struck a ridge and exploded. In that instant, McGovern and Buford may have become the first American casualties of the Vietnam War.

Under the CIA, the airline eventually became known as Air America and joined an expanding war in Vietnam, where, in the words of historian William M. Leary Jr. it would "pay a price in blood that would make [Dien Bien Phu] pale in comparison."

Later in 1954, after the subsequent French defeat by the Communist Vietminh forces and the partitioning of French Indochina into North and South Vietnam, Chennault again

Shown here is a C-119 Flying Boxcar dropping supplies to embattled troops. In 1950 the CIA took ownership of the CAT and used the Boxcars to support troops in Korea and later in Vietnam.

returned to the United States on a mission. His task this time was to rally support for his proposal for a 470-member International Volunteer Group (IVG) to be modeled on his highly successful American Volunteer Group. The old warrior intended the IVG to be used to stem the spreading threat of Communism in Southeast Asia without the direct involvement of the United States. He managed to attract the interest of a few important people in the military and political arenas but to little avail. Opposing factions in the Departments of State and Defense finally squelched his efforts. Chennault would lead no more.

In 1956, "the year of the cough," as Anna Chennault termed it, the general's health started to decline. A physical examination at Walter Reed Army Hospital in Washington revealed a malignant tumor on his left lung—cancer. (Chennault was an inveterate cigarette smoker.) "General Chennault received with rock-like fortitude," wrote Anna later, "the news that death would claim him in six months."

When asked by a friend what he intended to do about his cancer, Chennault said, "Do? Why I'm going to try and outlive it. If the Lord gives me enough time, I'll beat this one, too." And without fret or resignation, he began his last battle.

Chennault made the most out of the time remaining to him. He took Anna on a belated honeymoon to Europe, returning to Taiwan in time to celebrate the CAT's 10th anniversary. At the anniversary party, friends sadly watched Chennault, then too weak to cut the cake. The Chennaults left for the United States right after the party, arriving in San Francisco on January 10, 1958. The general's days were dwindling rapidly.

Little more than six months later, the greatest Flying Tiger of them all died in the Ochsner Foundation Hospital in New Orleans on Sunday, July 27, 1958. His death came only two days after having been appointed to lieutenant general (retired) by President Dwight D. Eisenhower. The appointment pleased Chennault greatly. But it had come too late.

★   ★   ★

Lieutenant General Claire Lee Chennault of the United States Air Force was buried with full military honors in the National Cemetery in Arlington, Virginia. He was a man born to do such things as others only dream of—and he did them.

1893

September 6   Claire Lee Chennault is born in Commerce, Texas.

1917

November 27   Commissioned a first lieutenant in the U.S. Army's infantry reserve at Fort Benjamin Harrison, Indiana.

1920

April 16   Discharged from the U.S. Army as a fighter pilot.

July 1   Accepting a regular commission as a first lieutenant in the new Air Service, Chennault reports to Ellington Field, Texas, to undergo training in the army's first course in aerial fighting tactics.

1923–1926   Chennault commands the Nineteenth Fighter Squadron—the "Fighting Cocks"—at Luke Field, Pearl Harbor, Hawaii, where he begins to develop his visionary view on fighter tactics.

1926–1931   Promoted to captain and assigned to Brooks Field, Texas, as a flight instructor, Chennault continues to develop and test his theories on aerial warfare.

1931–1937   Graduates from the Air Corps Tactical School at Langley Field, Virginia, and stays on at Langley as an instructor. He continues to advance his ideas and writes a treatise on *The Role of Defensive Pursuit*. As the founding member of "Three Men on a Flying Trapeze," an aerial acrobatic team, Chennault performs in air shows all around the country.

1937

April 30   Retires from the U.S. Army Air Corps with the rank of captain.

May 1   Heads to San Francisco to embark for China and an advisory position with the Chinese Air Force (CAF).

July 7   Japanese forces attack the Chinese garrison at Marco Polo Bridge in Lugouqiao, China; the "China Incident" or the Chinese "War of Resistance" begins.

July 9   Chennault offers his services to Chiang Kai-shek.

July 14   "Black Saturday"; Chinese bombers mistakenly bomb Shanghai.

1937–1940   Chennault directs the activities of the CAF in its war against Japan using Chinese and mercenary pilots and antiquated aircraft. He returns to the United States in October 1940 to procure pilots and planes.

1941   During the summer and fall, pilots of the newly formed American Volunteer Group (AVG)—better known as the "Flying Tigers"—arrive in Burma and undergo training by Chennault.

December 7   Japanese forces attack American bases in Pearl Harbor and the Philippines.

December 20   AVG pilots engage the Japanese for the first time over Iliang, China.

December 25   AVG pilots score a major victory against Japanese bombers and fighters over Rangoon on Christmas Day.

1942

April 15   The army reinstates Chennault in the U.S. Army Air Force as a brigadier general.

July 4   The AVG is disbanded. In barely more than six months of fighting, the Flying Tigers of the AVG destroy 299 Japanese planes in the air and another 153 probables.

July 5   The China Air Task Force (CATF), comprising the Twenty-third Fighter Group and the Eleventh Bombardment Squadron, replaces the AVG.

1943

March 10   President Franklin D. Roosevelt dissolves the CATF and creates the China-based Fourteenth Air Force with Chennault at its head; Chennault receives the second star of a major general.

May 11–25   Trident Conference held in Washington, D.C.

June   Chennault's air offensive begins. The Fourteenth Air Force destroys more than 2,600 Japanese planes and another 1,500 probables, sinks 44 ships, knocks out 600 bridges, and wipes out nearly 67,000 enemy troops.

1945

August 8   Chennault leaves China.

September 2   Japan formally surrenders.

October 31   Chennault retires from the U.S. Army Air Force.

1947

January 31   First flight of the China Air Transport (CAT), founded by Chennault and Whiting Willaeur.

1950   The Central Intelligence Agency acquires the CAT and uses it in support of United Nations forces in Korea (and eventually in support of French and U.S. operations in Vietnam under the name of Air America).

1958

July 27   Chennault dies in New Orleans.

Books

Bond, Charles B., and Terry H. Anderson. *A Flying Tiger's Diary.* College Station: Texas A & M University Press, 1984.

Boyington, Gregory. *Baa Baa Black Sheep.* New York: Putnam, 1958.

Byrd, Martha. *Giving Wings to the Tiger.* Tuscaloosa: University of Alabama Press, 1987.

Chambers, John Whiteclay, II, ed. *The Oxford Companion to American Military History.* New York: Oxford University Press, 1999.

Chennault, Anna. *The Education of Anna.* New York: Times Books, 1980.

————. *Chennault and the Flying Tigers.* New York: Paul S. Eriksson, 1963.

Chennault, Claire L. *Way of a Fighter.* New York: Putnam, 1949.

Cornelius, Wanda, and Thayne Short. *Ding Hao: America's Air War in China 1937-1945.* Gretna, LA: Pelican, 1980.

Dear, I. C. B., and M. R. D. Foot, eds. *The Oxford Companion to World War II.* New York: Oxford University Press, 1995.

Dupuy, R. Ernest, and Trevor N. Dupuy. *The Encyclopedia of Military History: From 3500 B.C. to the present.* Rev. ed. New York: Harper and Row, 1977.

Dupuy, Trevor N., Curt Johnson, and David L. Bongard. *The Harper Encyclopedia of Military Biography.* New York: HarperCollins, 1992.

Ford, Daniel. *Flying Tigers: Claire Chennault and the American Volunteer Group.* Washington, DC: Smithsonian Institution Press, 1991.

Hessen, Robert, ed. *General Claire Lee Chennault: A Guide to His Papers in the Hoover Institution Archives.* Hoover Press Bibliography Series 65. Stanford: Hoover Institution Press, 1983.

Leary, William M., Jr. *Perilous Missions.* Tuscaloosa, AL: University of Alabama Press, 1984.

Longyard, William H. *Who's Who in Aviation History: 500 Biographies.* Novato, CA: Presidio Press, 1994.

Maurer, Maurer. *Aviation in the U.S. Army, 1919-1939.* Washington, D.C.: Office of Air Force History, United States Air Force, 1987.

Moser, Don. *China-Burma-India.* Alexandria, VA: Time-Life, 1978.

Nalty, Bernard. *Tigers Over Asia.* New York: Elsevier-Dutton, 1978.

Polmar, Norman, and Thomas B. Allen. *World War II: The Encyclopedia of the War Years 1941-1945.* New York: Random House, 1996.

Rearden, Jim. *Cracking the Zero Mystery: How the U.S. Learned to Beat Japan's Vaunted World War II Fighter Plane.* Harrisburg, PA: Stackpole Books, 1990.

Scott, Robert L., Jr. *Flying Tiger: Chennault of China.* Garden City, NY: Doubleday, 1959.

Schultz, Duane. *The Maverick War: Chennault and the Flying Tigers.* New York: St. Martin's Press, 1987.

Seagrave, Sterling, and the Editors of Time-Life Books. *Soldiers of Fortune.* Alexandria, VA: Time-Life Books, 1981.

Smith, R. T. *Tale of a Tiger.* Van Nuys, CA: Tiger Originals, 1986.

Szuscikiewicz, Paul. *Flying Tigers.* New York: Gallery Books, 1990.

Tuchman, Barbara. *Stilwell and the American Experience in China, 1911–1945.* New York: Macmillan, 1971.

Tucker, Spencer C. *Who's Who in Twentieth-Century Warfare.* New York: Routledge, 2001.

Whelan, Russell. *The Flying Tigers: The Story of the American Volunteer Group.* Garden City, NY: Doubleday, 1942.

Periodicals

Grant, Rebecca. "Flying Tiger, Hidden Dragon." *Air Force Magazine,* March 2002, pp. 70-77.

Ayling, Keith. *Old Leatherface of the Flying Tigers: The Story of General Chennault.* New York: Bobbs-Merrill, 1945.

Caidin, Martin. *Zero Fighter.* New York: Ballantine Books, 1970.

———. *The Ragged, Rugged Warriors.* New York: E. P. Dutton, 1966.

Costello, John. *The Pacific War.* New York: Quill, 1982.

Greenlaw, Olga S. *The Lady and the Tigers.* New York: E. P. Dutton, 1943.

Hahn, Emily. *Chiang Kai-shek: An unauthorized biography.* Garden City, NY: Doubleday, 1955.

Horikoshi, Jiro, trans. by Shojiro Shindo and Harold N. Wantiez. *The Eagles of Mitsubishi: The Story of the Zero Fighter.* Seattle: University of Washington Press, 1981.

Koenig, William J. *Over the Hump: Airlift to China.* New York: Ballantine Books, 1972.

Leary, William M., Jr. *The Dragon's Wings.* Athens: University of Georgia Press, 1976.

Miller, Milt. *Tiger Tales.* Manhattan, KS: Sunflower University Press, 1984.

Okumiya, Masatake, and Jiro Horikoshi. *Zero!* New York: E. P. Dutton, 1956.

Pistole, Larry M. *The Pictorial History of the Flying Tigers.* Orange, VA: Moss Publications, 1981.

Sakai, Saburo. *Samurai!* New York: E. P. Dutton, 1957.

Samson, Jack. *Chennault.* Garden City, NY: Doubleday, 1987.

Scott, Robert L., Jr. *The Day I Owned the Sky.* New York: Bantam Books, 1988.

———. *God Is My Co-pilot.* New York: Scribner's, 1943.

Smith, Felix. *China Pilot: Flying for Chiang and Chennault.* Washington, DC: Brassey's, 1995.

Smith, Robert M., with Philip D. Smith. *With Chennault in China: A Flying Tiger's Diary*. Blue Ridge Summit, PA: TAB, 1984.

Sperry, Roland, with Terryl C. Boodman. *China Through the Eyes of a Tiger*. New York: Pocket Books, 1990.

Toland, John. *The Rising Sun: The Decline and Fall of the Japanese Empire, 1936-1945*. Vols. 1 and 2. New York: Random House, 1970.

Earle Rice Jr. is a former senior design engineer and technical writer in the aerospace industry. After serving nine years with the U.S. Marine Corps, he attended San Jose City College and Foothill College on the San Francisco Peninsula. He has devoted full time to his writing since 1993 and has written more than three dozen books for young adults. Earle is a member of the Society of Children's Book Writers and Illustrators; the League of World War I Aviation Historians and its UK-based sister organization, Cross & Cockade International, the United States Naval Institute, and the Air Force Association.